Multi-Sensory World

MULTI-SENSORY WORLD by Craig Borlase

Scripture Union, 207–209 Queensway, Bletchley, MK2 2EB, UK

email: info@scriptureunion.org.uk

www.scriptureunion.org.uk

Scripture Union Australia: Locked Bag 2, Central Coast Business Centre, NSW 2252

www.su.org.au

ISBN 978 1 84427 266 2

First published in Great Britain by Scripture Union 2008

Cover design by waldonwhitejones of Basildon, Essex, UK

Internal page design by Creative Pages: www.creativepages.co.uk

Some internal illustrations by Andy Gray: www.onegraydot.co.uk, using photographs with permission of Tearfund, taken by Jim Loring, Richard Hanson and Geoff Crawford in Cambodia, Niger, Burkina Faso, Sierra Leone and Kenya.

Printed and bound in Singapore by Tien Wah Press

Scripture Union is an international Christian charity working with churches in more than 130 countries providing resources to bring the good news about Jesus Christ to children, young people and families – and to encourage them to develop spiritually through the Bible and prayer. As well as coordinating a network of volunteers, staff and associates who run holidays, church-based events and school Christian groups, Scripture Union produces a wide range of publications and supports those who use their resources through training programmes.

Multi-Sensory World

Global issues explored – for creative churches,
youth groups and small groups

Craig Borlase

Contents

Page

Making the most of Multi-Sensory World   **7**

A personal word   **9**

1   **What's wrong with the world?**   Isaiah 58   **15**
A session about global injustice

2   **What's so special about God's kingdom?**   Luke 9:57–62   **18**
A session about finding focus

3   **Where do we fit in all this?**   Genesis 18:22–33   **21**
A session about each of us getting involved

4   **What's holding us back?**   Judges 13–16   **26**
A session about us and them in a me-first frenzy

5   **Which way is up?**   Job 29:7–17   **30**
A session about what Job teaches us about true faith

6   **How loudly do we have to sing?**   Amos 5; Isaiah 1:10–20   **34**
A session about worship and justice

7   **Are we nearly there yet?**   Exodus 16:4–30   **42**
A session about our journey

8   **Does my faith look big in this?**   Proverbs 29:7; Amos 8:4–6   **48**
A session about what we wear

9   **Why does my wallet ache?**   Matthew 6:19–34; 1 Timothy 6:3–19; James 5:1–5   **52**
A session about trade and hope

10   **Where are God's fingerprints?**   Psalm 65   **57**
A session about climate change, poverty and us

Case studies 1–7   **61**

Takeaways 1–10   **68**

This publication is a partnership project with Tearfund, who have provided the case study material from real mission stories from around the world.

Tearfund is a Christian relief and development agency working with a global network of local churches to help eradicate poverty. Their 10-year vision is to see 50 million people released from material and spiritual poverty through a worldwide network of 100,000 local churches.

www.tearfund.org

Making the most of Multi-Sensory World

We all need to grow as Christians and studying the Bible is a vital part of that growth. However, all too often, Bible study can degenerate into dreariness or study groups slide into cosy social gatherings. The *Multi-Sensory* series is designed to breathe life and vitality into the process of maturing in Christ, as well as deepening fellowship and helping everyone move faith into action.

Multi-Sensory World is aimed at helping creative groups in various settings explore what the Bible has to say about some vital and challenging global issues.

Reading the Bible

Remember that not everyone finds it easy to find their way around the Bible, so give people plenty of time to find passages and look up references. You will find it helpful to vary the way the Bible is read in the group or service, and think about using different Bible versions and ways of presenting the passage visually and aurally.

Using the material *your* way

If you want to focus on global issues for a period of time in your church or small group, you can work consecutively through all 10 sessions, selecting the material that best suits you. If your timetable or church programme doesn't allow for 10 sessions, be selective. Or you may wish to use the material to put on a week or weekend with special emphasis on world challenges, perhaps including an invitation to a guest speaker.

The sessions in **Multi-Sensory World** are built around a common 'menu' approach, but note that the sessions don't always work through them in the same sequence.

 ## Getting connected (allow 10–15 minutes)

This icebreaker will get everyone involved and sharing together from the very beginning. It is easy to see the value of this part of a session when a group is just starting out or when new people have recently joined, but even if you have known each other for a long time you will often be surprised at what you discover.

 ## Touching God (allow 15–20 minutes)

Jesus encouraged his followers to engage with God through all their senses. For example:

> **Look** at the birds of the air – Matthew 6:26.
>
> My sheep **listen** to my voice – John 10:27.
>
> **Touch** me and see – Luke 24:39.
>
> Take and **eat**; this is my body – Matthew 26:26.
>
> She has done a beautiful thing (when Mary poured sweet-**smelling** perfume over Jesus) – Mark 14:6.

So that's the emphasis of this part of the session.

 ## Living Scripture (allow 40–45 minutes)

The aim is to search the Scriptures, but also to allow the Scriptures to search us. 'All Scripture is God-breathed and is useful for teaching, rebuking, correcting and training in righteousness' (2 Timothy 3:16). Take a few moments to pray that God will inspire your discussion before you consider the questions.

Reaching out (allow 15–20 minutes)

It is easy to skip over this part of the meeting, particularly if you have let an earlier section run on too long. A group that stops looking outwards will soon become stagnant.

 Digging deeper

This is the optional 'homework' part of the evening for anyone who wants to continue to think about the theme between the sessions. It's supported by photocopiable sheets for the leader to give out for people to take away.

Preparing well

Each session in **Multi-Sensory World** includes a choice of material. Look ahead and decide which of the suggestions are right for your group. Many of the ideas require advance preparation – sometimes needing to be done not just the night before but over a period of weeks. Have everything ready before people arrive so you can concentrate on making them welcome. Don't be afraid to use the material as a springboard for your own ideas – adding your own touches, mixing and matching activities to suit your group.

Sharing the leadership

Sharing out responsibility for different parts of the meeting will strengthen the group. Work towards a rota where different people lead different sections each time. Meet in various homes so that everyone has the opportunity to give hospitality. Appoint an assistant leader and let them run the meeting from time to time. After all, if the group becomes too big to fit into one home, your assistant can start a second group!

Being people-minded

Be people-minded rather than programme-driven. Being welcoming is important. Timing is also important; start promptly and don't overrun. If you go on too late, people might think twice about coming back next time. Be aware of the quieter members and draw them in with a simple but direct question sometimes, such as, 'Chris, what do you think?' But be sensitive. If someone doesn't turn up, get in touch before the next meeting. The aim is not to pressurise people, but to let them know they matter. Pray regularly – daily if possible – for the members of your group.

Finally

Many of the ideas in **Multi-Sensory World** can be used effectively in all sorts of gatherings, large and small. You'll find most can be adapted for school assemblies, retreats, quiet days, camps, conferences, training events, student outreach, church services, prayer meetings, etc. Step out and experiment. Let your imagination fly!

A personal word

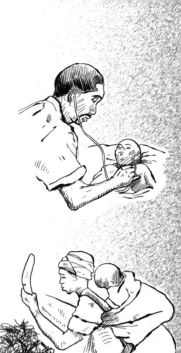

We live in impressive times. We're able to travel further and faster, communicate more clearly and creatively; and chart the course of our lives with greater accuracy and ambition.

But if we are able to do all this stuff, why does this world ache so much?

Why do more than a billion people worldwide lack clean water? Why, by 2050, will there be 150 million more people forced to leave their homes because of natural disasters caused by climate change? Why – when modern drugs slash the risk of mother-to-child transmission – is one baby born with HIV every minute? And why for every minute that passes do five people die because of AIDS? Why is it that unjust trade rules rob poor countries of £1.3 billion every day – 14 times more than they receive in aid?

If we're so impressive, why can we hear the earth groan like this?

I'd like to tell you a story. It starts with the words, 'I was visiting a slum in Mumbai, India… ' but I don't want you to get the wrong impression. I'm not one of those well-travelled writers who have a severely battered passport and a personal anecdote for every occasion. This trip was my first to a developing nation and I'd been waiting a long time for it to come around. So I was a little excited, to say the least, and had prepared fully for what I was convinced would be my reactions: a large dose of guilt at western extravagance and a side serving of impotence. But I was wrong. Very wrong…

* * *

I was visiting a slum in Mumbai, India. It was the last day of the trip and up to that point I'd been experiencing what I'd been told were the usual first-time reactions to the country: I was a little overwhelmed by the sights, sounds, smells and chaos; mildly anxious about the prospect of coming down with food poisoning; and totally petrified by the high-speed taxi rides. But it was not until I was gently sweating in front of a classroom full of 79 smiling, singing, praying children that I realised I was experiencing something that would stay with me forever.

You see, finally it all made sense; at last I understood why Christianity and justice are two words that were made to sit together. It's a little embarrassing to admit it, but it was only as I sat there in the education and feeding centre for kids of commercial sex workers that I realised how truly impressive Christianity can be.

I was feeling inspired, encouraged, challenged and incredibly proud of the work of Christians like Ratnamala – a social worker unlike any I've ever met. Her tour of a handful of slum dwellings was a blend of Mother

Teresa and Princess Diana. 'Because of her we will be accepted,' explained the pastor who had brought us there; and he was right.

We met Indira – a mother of two kids both supported by the project – whose life was too private to share with a tourist like me. And Pushpa, who told me she wasn't a Christian but she was pleased her children had been helped. Ratnamala explained that the lives of these two women could well improve through the work with their children. Sadly, HIV may have other plans.

Ratnamala and her three colleagues work with kids who used to hide under beds while their mothers worked. She's in touch with the family of four surviving on 60 pence a day; with the 12-year-old coping with the aftershocks of rape; with the ageing man with no chance of paying for the medicine he needs for his failing sight; with the young couple whose dream is to move up the ladder, leaving the slums behind. She and her team try to influence the 'proxy husbands' – guys who are somewhere between the status of client, pimp and teenage boyfriend. Their girls no longer work with other men but the arrangement is more financial than emotional, as if the men have put a deposit down on a future purpose. To all these and more, the team offer love, support and the unswerving belief that these individuals whom life threatens to overwhelm are worth the very best that they can give.

I was left speechless – but convinced that I had seen the most impressive thing on earth.

* * *

There's a phrase doing the rounds at Tearfund: 'The local church is the hope of the world.'

It has a certain ring to it, don't you think? But it's more than a half-decent sound bite; it's the basis of most of what they do. It's the compass for a better future.

Tearfund is one of the UK's largest development and relief charities. I've been one of their freelance writers for some time. They're an incredible bunch: committed, passionate and humble. By supporting local projects around the world they have the privilege of seeing the incredible impact that donors' money can have on the lives of the poorest people. They understand the central importance of the pursuit of justice to the Christian life – although they hate to give the impression that they've got things sewn up.

What the local church can offer is something more than handouts or help that can be totted up on a balance sheet – not that handouts and help aren't needed; to our shame a gaping chasm of inequality has slashed our world in two. But there's something else that Christians can offer, something else that gets added to the mix, something else that lies behind this whole 'hope of the world' statement.

It's about volume. And it's about motivation. And it's about the fact that this is precisely what we were made for: to love God and love others and be a fully functioning part of this multi-sensory world. We were never meant to close our hearts to the world's problems any more than we were to close our eyes to its beauty. We were made to be connected. We were made to be 'the hope of the world'.

But only certain Christians, right? We're not all supposed to be that concerned or that involved with the lives of the poor, are we? Surely it's only the ones with the special calling, the ones living near extreme poverty that need to have their lives defined by it? Aren't we like a colony of bees, existing in a complex network of different roles and responsibilities where some of us look after the poor, others of us make the money? Isn't that right?

* * *

What follows is biased. The ten sessions you're holding now are designed to help you connect with the aches of the world. Through discussion and study, art and meditation, real life stories and hands-on practical action, these simple resources will – I hope – highlight the ways in which local churches are offering life and hope to the world today. And I hope it will draw you in, stirring you up, increasing your discomfort but leaving you inspired and resourced to take action. Tearfund doesn't deal in guilt – they'd far rather have action as their currency. So while each of these sessions deals with big issues, they also all offer simple steps which you can take to make a difference.

Craig Borlase
www.craigborlase.com

Before you begin...

What you do when you put down this book could be world-changing. Maybe you'll go and plump up the cushions on the sofa, or maybe you'll clamber over the sideboard to grab the spare mugs down from the top cupboard.

Matthew Frost (photo by Layton Thompson/Tearfund)

These little preparations for the meeting of your small group may seem like nothing at all. But I really believe that you are taking part in God's eternal master plan for the healing of the world.

You're not the only ones planning to meet together this week – or next week, or next month. All over the world Christians are gathering in their communities to share a cup of tea, a thought on a Bible passage, and a little bit of their lives.

Some of the people in these local church meetings are hungry and won't eat until tomorrow. Some are in mourning for their friends who've died from AIDS. Some have lost their children, tragically, needlessly, to treatable diseases such as malaria or diarrhoea.

The Church gets everywhere. So does the incredible love of Jesus, who modelled for us the perfect way to meet people's social, spiritual and practical needs. 'God has given us his solution,' says Pastor Cuthbert Gondwe of Malawi. 'It's the local church.' The answer to global poverty is not within us. It is us.

I really believe that each little gathering of Christians in their community is a channel for God to change the world. That's why mobilising the local church to take action is at the heart of Tearfund's vision – and why I'm so excited that you've picked up this book. It may not be easy, but grappling with global injustice isn't really an option.

It's what truly loving our neighbours is all about.

Matthew Frost
Chief executive, Tearfund

1 What's wrong with the world?

Isaiah 58

A session about global injustice

There are many ways in which we could highlight what is wrong with the world. We could make lists of morality issues – long ones, too. We could trawl the media, cut and paste stories and clips of societies in conflict where hope appears to be all but absent. We could take a walk around our streets and see the bitter fruits of boredom and isolation and materialism's false promises.

Or we could look in the Bible.

Even though more than a couple of millennia have passed since much of it was written, Scripture highlights a range of common concerns that we share today: plagues of selfishness, greed and isolation which leave communities divided and individuals abandoned. Then, as now, humanity is torn between our own concerns and those of others. In other words, thousands of years may have passed but we've yet to come up with any truly new ways of messing things up.

 Getting connected

Noise

Get everyone to talk at once, speaking for a minute about their day so far, but at the same time trying to listen to what others are saying. How much information can each person pick up?

Or

Favourite food

Arrange in advance for everyone to bring a small amount of their favourite snack with them and share it with others.

Or

Personally speaking

Ask a volunteer to read out loud **A personal word** from page 9. Have you ever visited a developing country? What are your most significant memories?

 Living Scripture – Isaiah 58

Catch us at our best and our actions and our words really do match. At our worst we say one thing and do another. Isaiah understood this. He saw the same troubles around him – and spoke out. Read Isaiah 58 out loud.

1 We're probably all familiar with many of the words here. We're probably a little numb to some of them too. As a starter, consider the first part of verse 3 where the worshippers wonder why, despite all their best efforts, God appears not to be listening. What have you been waiting for God to do, with little sign of his response?

2 Now move on to the rest of verse 3 and verse 4: the answer to the previous question. Just as Isaiah's audience needed to check their actions against their words, we need to consider our own lives. Is it at all possible, for example, that the way we shop, the way we dress and the way we bank contribute to or combat the injustice we sing about? Which scream loudest to God: our words or our actions?

3 Verses 6 and 7 move the focus on from our own errors towards our potential for good. These are practical, accessible tasks. Why are these simple deeds so powerful?

4 Re-read verses 10–12. The words given to Isaiah reveal the closeness of the relationship between our worship of God and our lifestyle. What God wants from us is a lifelong commitment to worship him and, in doing so, to love others. He wants more than promising words; he wants to see it all put into action. God wants us to step out of the bubble, break free from superficial and selfish values and start to live for something other than our own satisfaction. He wants us to live beyond our own wish lists. How do you feel about that?

5 At this point, you might be wondering: Aren't we supposed to be talking about what's wrong with the world? How come we've ended up on personal discrepancies, on the integrity issues of those of us in the Church? Shouldn't we be looking further afield? Remind yourselves again of the chapter's shift in tone from outlining our errors to highlighting our potential. Read verse 11 yet again. Isn't that a great simile? How much potential do we hold as 'well-watered gardens'? Over a third of the world's population describe themselves as Christians. Should we settle for anything less than the belief that together we hold the power to utterly transform our world?

 ## Touching God

Listening to the stones

You will need: some large sheets of paper – ideally a roll of white lining paper; plenty of felt-tip pens, highlighters, poster paints and brushes; a clock or timer, preferably with a loud tick; a bucket containing bricks, stones or pebbles; a waterproof sheet to protect the floor.

Take some sheets of paper and create a large cross shape on the floor. Nominate one person to sit next to the bucket of stones and the timer, transferring the stones one at a time to make a pile on the floor at the rate of five per minute (that's every 12 seconds if you're struggling to find the calculator!).

Invite everyone else – in silence – to watch and listen to the sound and rhythm of the growing pile of stones. Tell them that with every stone, somewhere in the world, another person has died of an AIDS-related illness. And with every stone another four children have died, somewhere in the world, as a result of extreme – and avoidable – poverty.

Look at the cross. Was life really meant to be this way?

Invite everyone to pick up a pen or a brush and approach the cross and, on their knees, to write or paint in words or pictures their prayers of repentance.

Continue to listen to the stones.

 ## Reaching out

Hope in Uganda

Think about the incredible potential of Christians. At times, focusing on our own shortcomings makes it hard to see the possibilities. Give out photocopies of **Hope in Uganda** (page 61) and read together to find out how some Christians are transforming their communities.

Possible responses, now and ongoing:

Pray for the work of the Uganda Women Concern Ministry, those it helps and others living with AIDS worldwide. Learn more by visiting www.bepartofamiracle.org.uk/Resources.

Arrange a showing in your church of some short films from Tearfund on how local churches are providing hope in the midst of the AIDS crisis. You can find them at www.tearfund.org/bringchildhoodbacktolife.

 Digging deeper

Give out copies of **Takeaway 1** (page 68), encouraging people to read it before the next session.

2 What's so special about God's kingdom?

Luke 9:57–62

A session about finding focus

God's kingdom has no borders or guards, no fence or maps. But when Jesus taught his followers how to pray, we are left with some indications of how it works:

> *'your kingdom come,*
> *your will be done,*
> *on earth as it is in heaven.'*
>
> Matthew 6:10

God's kingdom is intrinsically linked to his will; it grows as we carry out the tasks we have been given. Loving God, loving our neighbour, choosing something other than self first; these are the signs of the kingdom of God. As much as God is mysterious and beyond our understanding, his kingdom is signposted by practical, tangible and often visible acts of kindness, love and sacrifice.

In this session we will wonder how we can be a part of it.

 Getting connected

Jewels

Take turns to describe a special item you value – perhaps a piece of jewellery or a favourite ornament, an item of furniture or a book. What makes it significant to you?

Or

Fantasy

Remember your childhood fantasies? Tell each other about the jobs you wanted to do, the games you used to play or the kingdoms you wanted to create.

 Living Scripture – Luke 9:57–62

This passage is a trio of encounters where people misunderstand the true cost of discipleship. The first person jumps in without being called. The second – the mate with the corpse in the deep freeze! – can't seem to get free of the law. The third says he'll follow God but attaches conditions as if it is some grand career move which he can only complete once all the loose ends are tied up.

All of them miss the point about our part in God's kingdom and Luke doesn't tell us whether any of them come good in the end.

1 Read Luke 9:57–62. What could Jesus have meant by what he said in verse 60? Then read John 5:24,25. Is Jesus referring to the physically dead? Or is he talking about the spiritually dead? Is he talking literally? Or metaphorically?

2 If Jesus is saying that his followers should let the spiritually dead take care of the physically dead, what does this imply about the importance he places on burial ritual? Is Jesus anti-

burial? Should we be protesting outside funeral homes and cemeteries? Why not? What's really going on here?

3   Disciples were expected to follow their rabbis, but the request to go and bury his father (Luke 9:59) is surely not that outrageous. Burial was an important ritual that the religious observed diligently. But Jesus appears to be raising the stakes here, suggesting that the rituals are less important than might be thought. What do you think Jesus is saying?

4   Jesus says to the man: 'Follow me ... proclaim the kingdom of God.' The word translated as 'follow' (akoloutheo) appears 76 times in the Gospels, mainly as 'follow' and often as the kind of following that was done by a disciple. It implies a journey with a purpose, not merely an aimless wander. The idea that someone could follow and proclaim (declare or preach) the kingdom (the royalty and rule) of God, suggests that Jesus is making the proposition of a lifetime. Does the same proposition – not an abstract concept but a tangible relationship with Jesus in which following him matters more than anything else – apply to us? How uncomfortable does that make you feel?

 Touching God

Barriers to Christ

You will need: four objects which symbolise the barriers discussed below. You could use an egg timer or a running stopwatch to represent impetuousness; a hammer and nail to represent ritual; a mirror to represent arrogance; and a rock to represent death. Use your imagination to find alternatives if these aren't available. Also: candles (being aware, of course, of safety precautions); quiet instrumental music (both optional).

The Bible passage showed us some potential barriers to being a part of God's kingdom: being impetuous, taking a slavish approach to ritual and religion or having an over-inflated sense of our own worth. And there's that big barrier of death; some of us feel spiritually dead inside – so much so that God feels utterly distant and remote.

Set up your four symbols in the four corners of the room or in whatever spaces you can create. Dim the lighting and use candles and music to create a reflective atmosphere. Invite people to move quietly from station to station in whatever order they like; or they can spend the whole time at one station if they prefer.

Encourage people to use the time and the props to think about how they respond to Jesus' call, 'Follow me.'

 Reaching out

Breaking down barriers in Ethiopia

When we choose to follow Jesus he will always lead us out – away from the comfort of religious ritual and towards the lives of those in need. Give out photocopies of **Breaking down barriers in Ethiopia** (page 62) and read it through quietly.

Possible responses, now and ongoing:

– Think about where God is calling you to follow him. It might not be at all far from where you are… so talk about the areas of need you are aware of in your neighbourhood. How would your area look different if the kingdom of God impacted it some more?

– We all need to hear the call to follow Jesus – but for some it requires a bigger change of direction than others. Being sensitive to that, allow people time and space to talk and pray things through.

Digging deeper

Give out copies of **Takeaway 2** (page 69), encouraging people to read it before the next session.

3 Where do we fit in all this?

Genesis 18:22–33

A session about each of us getting involved

The kingdom of God grows as a result of our taking Jesus up on his offer to follow him. Session 2 addressed that issue, while this session takes a look at a similar subject from a different angle: our responsibility.

In his book *To Heal A Fractured World*, Chief Rabbi of the Commonwealth and Britain Dr Jonathan Sacks describes the presence of justice within the world in two categories: divine and human. The divine, he says, is God's prerogative. We cannot force it, emulate it, or recreate it; it is above and beyond our comprehension and our prediction. But human justice – now, that's another story altogether. Only we can create it; only our hands can make it.

 Getting connected

Viewing

Watch a clip from near the end of the awarding-winning film about the fate of the Jews in Europe in the Second World War, *Schindler's List,* when Oscar Schindler claims, 'I could have done more.' If you can't get hold of the DVD, you can find it on YouTube.

Or

Sitting in cooperation

Stand in a circle facing the back of the person in front of you. At the signal, have everyone sit down onto the lap of the person behind. It might take a few goes to get it right, but it's pretty good when you do!

 Living Scripture – Genesis 18:22–33

Divine justice is appealing. The human variety takes more effort and opens us up to the risk of failure… and humiliation… and hard work. Yet the Bible makes the message clear: we are meant to be involved. We are meant to act. We are meant to be agents of human justice on the earth.

1 Read the Genesis passage. What's your response to the sequence in which Abraham barters with God? Are you comfortable with the idea that we can haggle with the Almighty?

2 What happens next? Skim read Genesis 19. The angels visit the city, the citizens try to rape them, and only four decent, righteous people are found. The city gets destroyed, just as God suggested it would, even before Abraham started bargaining. Why did God let Abraham go through the negotiations? As the omnipresent Creator, the all-seeing, almighty One, surely God knew that Abraham's figure of ten was too high and that the city would end up trashed anyway? Why go through the motions?

Personally, I think that God wanted Abraham to ask, to get involved, to care about the state of his fellow man. Why? Because that is precisely how we've been made; in the image of our God who cares passionately about the state of the world. We're not here to soak up the blessing and ignore the responsibilities. We're here to offer an accompaniment to God's divine justice:

human justice. We're supposed to get involved; we're supposed to feel, to ask questions and rage against a world plagued by the marks of the fall.

3   What would a world devoid of human justice look like? Would God be absent?

4   Have a look at Amos 7:1–17. Can you see anything familiar there? Is there a link between the way Amos and Abraham intervene? Why is this about more than just prayer? Why does human justice rely on our actions as well as our intercessions?

5   Can you think of any other parts of the Bible which follow this theme of humanity's flip-flopping between accepting and ignoring responsibilities?

 Touching God

You will need: a photocopy of **Jars of clay** from page 24, perhaps enlarged and/or coloured; a copy of **The jars of clay script** from page 25; a bucket of wet clay or garden soil (not too sloppy or you'll have a lot of mess to clean up); one or more bowls of warm soapy water; towels; a sheet of plastic to protect the flooring.

Pin the photocopy prominently above the bucket and bowls and choose a good reader to use the script, reading slowly and with appropriate pauses as people follow the actions.

 Reaching out

It is tempting to think that we don't have the tools to care for others in practical ways. It is tempting to think that our hands are too dirty or weak, our lives too local, our influence too small really to affect change.

This is wrong.

Our lives are always ripe for being involved in the kingdom of God. For just as the call to follow Christ is spoken to all, so can all take up the mantle of human justice.

Give out photocopies of **Filling empty hands in Malawi** on page 63 and read it through quietly.

Possible responses, now and ongoing:
–   Encourage everyone to think about something simple that they feel they could do to help someone but have not yet got around to. It might be buying or cooking a meal for someone, giving money to a needy charity, sending a card or email to someone who's lonely or bereaved.

–   Think about joining an organisation that campaigns for others.

–   Could you write to your MP as individuals or as a group about the needs of the local community?

–   Ask yourself if there is a change to your lifestyle you could make which would directly benefit someone else. Could you commit to that change and ask someone else in the group to help you be accountable over the next few weeks?

–   Take a look at www.tearfund.org/campaigning. Is there an action there that you can take? Or could you set yourself a target of recruiting three others outside the group to get involved?

Digging deeper

Give out copies of **Takeaway 3** (page 70), encouraging people to read it before the next session.

JaRS of Clay

'In the village there was a belief that if I am lacking then I cannot assist anyone. But we told people that in the midst of lacking there is still something that I can assist my friend with.'

Pastor Harry, Fombe, Malawi

For we do not preach ourselves, but Jesus Christ as Lord, and ourselves as your servants for Jesus' sake. For God, who said, "Let light shine out of darkness," made his light shine in our hearts to give us the light of the knowledge of the glory of God in the face of Christ.

But we have this treasure in jars of clay to show that this all-surpassing power is from God and not from us. We are hard pressed on every side, but not crushed; perplexed, but not in despair; persecuted, but not abandoned; struck down, but not destroyed.

2 Corinthians 4:5–9

The jars of clay script

One at a time, put both your hands into the bucket and feel the mud. Experience the texture. Take your hands out. Take a long, hard look at them. Stand in a circle around the bucket as others do the same.

Now that everyone has muddy hands, ask yourself: Do you feel ready to go and cook? To use your phone? To take your keys out of your pocket? To shake someone else by the hand? To pick up a child? To sit at your desk to work?

Dirty hands make us feel unable to function in anything like the way we function with clean hands.

Now ask yourself: When I'm lacking, am I really unable to help others?

Close your eyes. Take time to talk to God in this short silence about the ways in which you feel inadequate… the ways you often feel unable to help… the times when you are too busy… or perhaps when you feel too poor… too stressed… too far away… too broken.

Now open your eyes and read the quotations a few times over.

Our hands may be dirty, our security fragile, our resources low… but it is God who provides, in spite of our weakness.

It's time to wash your hands now.

4 What's holding us back?

Judges 13–16

A session about us and them in a me-first frenzy

In this session we're going to turn our minds to what it is that holds us back from getting involved in issues of global justice. How come, in this truly multi-sensory world, we are tempted to spend so much time looking inward rather than looking outward? Is this all down to the pressures of life in the twenty-first century? Can the Bible offer any helpful insights?

Well, the good news is that Scripture presents any number of examples of characters falling into the same trap that we often do. Take Samson, for example. He was born at a time when the Israelites were locked in a repeating cycle of rebellion, judgement and deliverance. The situation was dire, with God's people suffering under the oppressive Philistine regime. Samson was born with a clear mandate, to free the Israelites and bring them back to God.

 ## Getting connected

Kim's Game revisited

You will need: a large tray; 10–15 assorted small objects from around the house; a blindfold.

Rehash the classic kids' party game. Blindfold someone and challenge them to try to guess the identity of a range of objects by touch alone. Or, alternatively, use objects that have to be identified using only their sense of smell. Or, take it to the next level if you dare, by providing a range of items that have to be identified solely using the sense of taste.

Or

Test of strength

You will need: a pile of A4 scrap paper.

Give each person a sheet of A4 and have them tear it in half, then place one half on top of the other before ripping both sheets in half again. Repeat as often as possible, each time doubling the number of sheets through which you are tearing. Who can tear the most number of times?

 ## Living Scripture – Judges 13–16

Samson's destiny was impressive. But as he grew up his life proved to be rather less so. What went wrong?

1   It's quite long, but skim read the story of Samson from start to finish. Here's an idea to bring it to life. Get a couple of kids' toys to represent the characters, such as an Action Man for Samson, a Barbie for Delilah. Two people from the group can act as puppet masters while the rest of you call out the main points of the action as you go through the story out loud and they try to portray the action.

2   Revisit Judges 13:5. An angel with a message for a childless woman; news of a son soon to be born; the promise of future deliverance for God's people – does that remind you of anything? Samson starts out in a pretty elite club, don't you think?

3   Check out Judges 14:2. If anyone's got a study Bible, they should have a note about the Philistine town of Timnah. It's clear that this young woman lived reasonably close to Samson's

home town of Zorah (about four miles away by some estimates). Is this proximity of risk and temptation symbolic of anything in Samson's heart? What rules did God have about Israelites marrying outside the community?

4 Take a closer look at Judges 14:13. These were serious outfits that Samson was gambling with; a man might expect to own only one of these during his entire lifetime. Again Samson's playing with fire. Why does he do it?

5 Judges 14:19 is a troubling verse. The first sentence suggests that God appears to be in some way supporting Samson on his 30-mile hike to a coastal town called Ashkelon where he murders, loots and pillages until he has enough cash to pay back the Philistines. Could God really be happy at this killing of 30 men? Why does he let it happen?

6 Judges 16:1 should be convincing for anyone in any doubt as to the extent of Samson's fall from grace. Where is God in these episodes?

7 Samson's final showdown scene remains the most well known. Here, in Gaza – the scene of his mighty and miraculous escape when he ran off with the city gates – Samson ends up a mere plaything, an oddity to be wheeled out when the crowd were nicely lubricated on afternoon booze. Judges 16:28 offers us the Bible's first and last record of Samson praying. That doesn't mean he didn't pray; but what kind of point do you think the author could be making here?

8 Samson's final days were spent blind, yet for his whole life he lacked insight into his own behaviour. He was unable to see that his habit of trusting in his own abilities and giving in to his own appetites was second best. His greatest achievement – as measured against his earlier promise of being the one to deliver the Israelites from the oppression of the Philistines – came in his death (Judges 16:30). Is there anything in this story that reminds you of the attitudes and values we often have? Do we spend too much time getting sidetracked by our own appetites? Are our actions marked more by selfish intent than a pursuit of divine intention? Is our potential for good a distant mirage?

 Touching God

Telling your story
You will need: photocopies of **My story** (page 29); plenty of plain paper; pens; felt-tip pens.

Samson's errors – the selfishness, the appetites that could not be ignored, the desire to ignore God – are familiar to us all. But they do not have to be our only option; they are not our default setting. Jesus made it clear that another way was possible.

Invite people to tell their own story – the account of how they have come to be where they are in their faith today. Offer people a choice of styles. They can use prose. They can produce a timeline. Or a flow chart. Or a spider diagram. Or a comic strip. Or they can use the supplied template. Invite them to use any method which helps them narrate the story of their journey so far.

Depending on your group, conclude by inviting some 'show and tell', encouraging people to describe their stories. Or you could do this in twos or threes.

If you have time, give out more paper and invite people to describe their onward faith journey as they'd like it to be. Get them to reflect on what it would take to make that happen.

Reaching out

Tackling trade in people in Cambodia

Turn the spotlight on people trafficking, a major global evil in our times.

Give out photocopies of **Tackling trade in people in Cambodia** (page 64) and read it through quietly before discussing your views.

Sitting comfortably at home in the wealthy West, it can seem as though the problems of trafficked children and other vulnerable people are a million miles away. What can we do about it? Aren't these problems that only politicians and overseas charities can really help out with?

Possible responses, now and ongoing:

– Think about getting involved with Tearfund's Children at Risk campaign (http://www.tearfund. org/childrenatrisk) which has made a significant impact on the lives of trafficked children. Over recent years, fund-raising has helped partners like CHO (Cambodia Hope Organisation) protect thousands of lives. In 53 countries around the world, tens of thousands of children are educated, housed, clothed, trained, counselled or simply looked after by people who care – people just like us – living thousands of miles away.

– None of us would really want to end up like Samson. It's a cautionary tale of wasted potential. One way forward is to be purposeful about wanting a life that is less selfish. Often progress is made in this in making small steps of love and sacrifice, making decisions to help others rather than gorge ourselves, making choices that will leave others freer from injustice rather than those that will leave us with a slightly polished ego. Can you think of something specific that would fit into one of those categories? Share your idea with someone in the group and plan to put it into action as soon as you can.

– Pray for CHO and similar organisations, for the people they help and for Christians worldwide who have such incredible power to support the vulnerable in this way.

 Digging deeper

Give out copies of **Takeaway 4** (page 71), encouraging people to read it before the next session.

My story...

5 Which way is up?

Job 29:7–17

A session about what Job teaches us about true faith

How important are we in the whole scheme of things? It might seem like an odd question, but it's a good one. After all, legions of advertisers would have us believe that we should purchase 'because we're worth it'. So how much are we worth? Put another way, how much do we deserve?

The story of Job in the Old Testament mulls over this question. It tells the story of a wealthy, God-fearing family man whose life gets turned inside out, apparently as a result of a bizarre battle of wills between God and the devil.

It's a strange story, but it can be illuminating about the nature of true faith.

But first… a little comedy.

 Getting connected

'Luxury!' 1
Search YouTube with the words 'Four Yorkshiremen' and watch the classic *Monty Python* sketch that looks at the nature of suffering and childhood hardship.

Or

'Luxury!' 2
Search Google with the words 'Four Yorkshiremen script' and print it off. Select four of your group to read it out. Award a prize (a 'luxury chocolate bar'?) as you all vote for the best accent.

 Living Scripture – Job 29:7–17

1 Working together as a group, remind each other of the story of Job – the wealth, the status, the faith, the bit with the devil in the garden, followed by the incredible suffering and those truly awful friends who offer so many words yet so little comfort. Talk about all the bizarre questions that come to mind when considering Job's story. Why do you think it is so different from other books of the Bible?

2 There's one question that drives the book: Why? Why does Job get singled out for such special treatment? Take a few minutes to see what different ideas you can all come up with as possible reasons.

3 Read Job 29:7–17. This is where we find Job musing over his past actions. Suddenly it becomes clearer for us: this is what righteousness looks like; this is the way that true faith acts; this is what God had in mind when he offered Job as an example of one whose faith was strong. Like Abraham and Amos, he assumes responsibility for righting the wrongs of a fallen society. He is an agent of human justice. What was it about Job's character that made him God's choice? (See also Job 1.)

4 Have volunteers in the group read out loud the following verses:

> Jeremiah 9:23,24
> Matthew 22:37

Mark 12:30
Luke 10:27
Deuteronomy 6:5
Leviticus 19:18

Discuss the picture that emerges of the way in which our lives are supposed to be distinctive.

5   Read Micah 6:8. Job surely understands the need for us to act justly, to love mercy, to walk humbly with our God, just as the prophet instructs. These are the true jewels of relationship with God: the determination to remain devoted whatever the weather; the actions of supporting, nurturing, protecting, and providing for those whose lives have been scarred as a consequence of a fallen world; the responsibility we have to submit to the mandate to love and serve God and others. There are so many biblical examples of these characteristics in flesh and bone, but none better, of course, than Jesus. Talk about the ways in which Jesus' words and actions were a perfect illustration of a lifestyle in line with God's wishes.

 Touching God

Fairtrade

You will need: some Fairtrade chocolate; a pair of scissors (optional).

Jesus lived his life in view of the poor – not hidden away among the trappings of wealth. Too often we want to do something to help fight poverty, but feel disconnected from those trapped by it. But global trading means that our lives are intricately connected with others living all across the world. This activity helps us think about trade and the ways that our choices in the high street can be used for greater good.

Start by reading out Proverbs 13:23:

> *A poor man's field may produce abundant food*
> *but injustice sweeps it away.*

Unjust trade rules rob poor countries of £1.3 billion every day. That's 14 times more than they receive in aid.

Have a look together at some of the labels in your clothes that tell you how to care for them and where they were made. Some of you might like to take the scissors, cut out some of those labels and lay them in front of the group. Talk about what the conditions might have been like for the people that made the clothes.

Spend some time in prayer, asking for changes to be made in government legislation and consumer habits that mean that garment manufacturers around the world would be paid a wage that means they can live and not simply survive.

Break the chocolate into squares and pass it around. As everyone puts theirs into their mouths, ask them to pray for farmers – many of whom provide our food but often can't afford to enjoy the taste of it.

Or

Jeremiah memory poster

You will need: photocopies of the posters on page 33; felt-tip pens.

Distribute the posters and colour them in silence, repeating the verses in your mind. Take the poster home and pin it up in a prominent place. Commit with each other to try to memorise the verses by the time you all next meet.

Reaching out

Dreams coming true in Bangladesh
Give out photocopies of **Dreams coming true in Bangladesh** (page 65) and read it through quietly before discussing your views.

Possible responses, now and ongoing:

- Try to imagine both the quantity and quality of the kind of transformation possible through the handicraft workshops. Thank God for Heed and the thousands of individuals whose lives have been helped by the work.

- Pray for those whose lives have been ripped from their tracks by war and conflict. From Darfur to Iraq, Afghanistan to the Congo and beyond, pray for those who face overwhelming troubles and fear. Pray that they would know God's presence with them, even in the darkest places.

- Pray for inspiration and boldness for your own life, that you too might be a peacemaker, a supporter and a carer to those in trouble.

Digging deeper

Give out copies of **Takeaway 5** (page 72), encouraging people to read it before the next session.

This is what the LORD says:

"Let not the wise man boast of his wisdom

or the strong man boast of his strength

or the rich man boast of his riches,

but let him who boasts boast about this:

that he understands and knows me,

that I am the LORD, who exercises kindness,

justice and righteousness on earth,

for in these I delight,"

declares the LORD.

Jeremiah 9:23,24

6 How loudly do we have to sing?

Amos 5; Isaiah 1:10–20

A session about worship and justice

There's a myth doing the rounds. It's nothing new; it's been in circulation for thousands of years. It goes a little like this: God likes it best when we're doing the religious ritual stuff really, really well. The Lord – so this myth would have us believe – has a discerning eye. Like an ageing monarch he knows exactly how things should and should not be done, and only the very best servants are able to carry out the routines with the requisite flair and care.

Rubbish.

You know it's rubbish, don't you? At some level we all do. We all know that Christianity has nothing to do with being impressive and a great deal to do with living obediently, sacrificially and with great love. But while we know this, there are times when the temptation to consider the Sunday service as the high point of our 'spiritual' week can be pretty strong.

God likes our worship, but it's not just about the songs. As Amos makes clear, our words are meaningless, putrid even, if they are not backed up by our actions. Surely – and I'm just guessing here – God likes our worship partly because it comes with some significant by-products? Surely at its best our worship goes beyond pleasant harmonies and musical appreciation? Surely true worship is a life devoted to God and his cares and concerns… with lives transformed as a result?

 Getting connected

Guesstimate Quiz 1

You will need: photocopies of the quiz on page 37; pens.

Give everyone five minutes to write their answers in the boxes and then compare your results. Who got the closest?

Answers:

1 6,468

2 About 70 hours. There are a little under 800,000 words in the Bible and the average reader can get through nearly 200 words per minute.

3 Idolatry and justice

4 10 per cent

Or

Guess that song

You will need: dried pea shakers or kazoos (optional).

This calls for a particularly robust sense of self-worth! Get volunteers to perform one of their favourite worship songs or hymns or even Sunday School choruses and see who can guess the words first. To perform the song they are limited to either (1) humming or (2) lah-lahing or (3) a kazoo or (4) a dried pea shaker.

Living Scripture – Amos 5; Isaiah 1:10–20

The Bible is practical. OK, so we might not be talking about tips on how to improvise an asparagus steamer or everyday stain removal in three easy steps. But when it comes to the important things – the life and death issues – the Bible's got it all in black and white.

1 There was no social security back in the days of tents, shepherds and papyrus scrolls. So God made it clear that the responsibility for relieving the crushing oppression of poverty lay with his own people. Have you ever heard of the Year of Jubilee? The **Digging deeper** section will give you more info, but meanwhile take a look at Deuteronomy 24:19–21. It explores the law of gleaning, a system where crops that were not collected at the first harvest were to be left for those who were in greater need. Why would God suggest this?

2 Read Amos 5:7,11,12. Of all the usual suspects, who could these words be describing? The Philistines? Ninevites? Egyptians? The answer is 'none of the above'. It is God's people, the Israelites, at whom these words are spat. How could this be?

3 Read Isaiah 1:10–20. This offers more insight into the mistakes made by God's own people. Talk about what particularly angers God. Should we be surprised by this?

4 Read Amos 5:21,22, where hypocrisy gets an even more thorough critique. Is this behaviour understandable to you? The chances are that it won't appear totally alien. So many of us act likewise – we get the sequence wrong much of the time.

5 Talk about people you know who live in ways that you admire; the ones whose actions and care for others surely make God pleased. Do you know what motivates them? What do they do that makes an impression on you?

 Touching God

Worship without words

You will need: an enlarged photocopy of **What the Lord requires** (page 38); a large sheet of thick white paper or cardboard; as big a variety of paints, brushes and marker pens as you can source; newspapers; scissors; glue; scraps of fabric; candles (optional; be aware of safety issues if you use them); instrumental music (optional).

Have someone read out Micah 6:8, while someone else takes the photocopy and glues it onto the centre of the paper or card. Working in silence, create a collage around the verse which represents your response to it. Doing this by candlelight and with peaceful music in the background may be helpful to create a meditative atmosphere.

To close this part of the session, say this prayer:

Father, if we spent our lives pouring out words to describe you,

We could still never come close to defining you.

All our words and songs and home-made beauty cannot do you justice,

Yet you are kind and gracious in accepting what we give.

Reaching out

Caring for orphans in Uganda

Words like those offered by Micah make sense. Another place to go for inspiration is James 1:27: 'Religion that God our Father accepts as pure and faultless is this: to look after orphans and widows in their distress and to keep oneself from being polluted by the world.' With that in your mind, give out and read in silence **Caring for orphans in Uganda** (page 66).

Will we choose to ignore the reality of child-headed households and leave it to the locals to clear up the mess? Or will we choose to do something about it?

Possible responses, now and ongoing:

— Pray specifically about the chaos that AIDS causes. Pray for the families decimated and left behind; for the carers struggling to cope; for local churches and Christians able to put words and actions together.

— Think about getting involved in practical help. Your donations can make a dramatic difference to the lives of those who have been left isolated and vulnerable by AIDS. Find out more at www.tearfund.org or by calling 0845 355 8355 and requesting the free 'Bring Childhood Back to Life' pack.

 Digging deeper

Give out copies of **Takeaway 6** (page 73), encouraging people to read it before the next session.

6 How loudly do we have to sing?

Guesstimate Quiz 1

Your answer

1. There are over 1,200 promises given in the Bible. How many commands does it contain?

2. How many hours would it take to read the entire Bible out loud?

3. What are the two most popular topics in the Old Testament?

4. What percentage of verses in the New Testament relate to money, justice or poverty?

8 Does my faith look big in this?

Guesstimate Quiz 2

Your answer

1. On average how much do we each spend on clothes each year in the UK?

2. How many pairs of shoes does the average American woman own?

3. What percentage of the world's garment workers are female?

4. What percentage of children between 4 and 14 in the developing world work?

5. In China you need to earn 50p per hour to maintain a basic standard of living. What do you think is the average pay for garment workers?

WHAT THE LORD REQUIRES

He has showed you … what is good.

And what does the LORD require of you?

To act justly and to love mercy

and to walk humbly with your God.

Micah 6:8

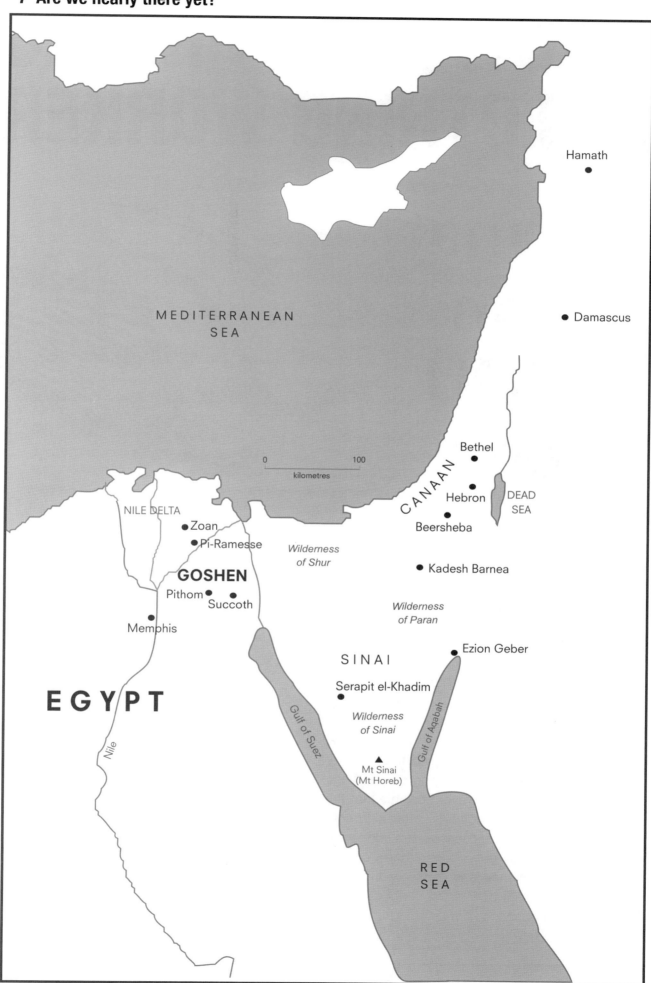

Hamath

MEDITERRANEAN
SEA

Damascus

0   100
kilometres

Bethel

C A N A A N

Hebron   DEAD
SEA

NILE DELTA

Zoan   Beersheba

Pi-Ramesse   *Wilderness
of Shur*

GOSHEN   Kadesh Barnea

Pithom   *Wilderness
of Paran*

Succoth

Memphis

Ezion Geber

S I N A I

E G Y P T   Serapit el-Khadim

Gulf of Suez   *Wilderness
of Sinai*   *Gulf of Aqabah*

Nile

▲
Mt Sinai
(Mt Horeb)

R E D
S E A

ACTION TO PROTECT CLOTHING WORKERS

What can YOU do?

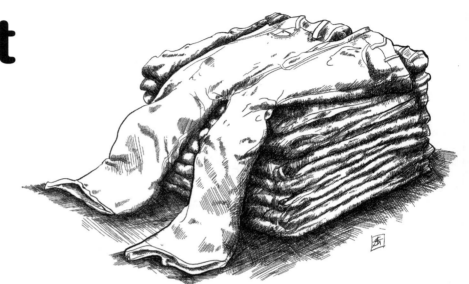

---

1 You can write

Find out the contact details of your favourite retailers and write to the CEO and Managing Directors; start a dialogue in which you encourage them to sign up to something called the Ethical Trading Initiative. This is a voluntary code that sees major retailers pledging to treat workers and suppliers fairly, paying proper wages and ensuring wherever possible that they work in safe conditions. After all, people running big businesses are driven by profit. If they get a sense that a growing number of their shoppers are interested in the stories behind the clothes, policies might change.

2 You can ask questions in the high street

Ask the staff in the stores if they can tell you where the clothes came from and what the working conditions are like. Ask the managers, too; get them talking and wondering about the supply chain for themselves. When you pay at the cash register, ask for a comment card and write that you would like the shops to join the Ethical Trading Initiative, to show that you care about those behind the products and that you want the shop to put people before profits.

3 You can pray

As Christians we have power and authority in Jesus' name to encourage and to pray and to ask our Father to let his kingdom come on this earth. As Christian consumers acting and praying together for justice, we really do have the power to make a huge difference.

4 You can shop ethically

We can make a conscious choice to buy stuff through ethical and Fair Trade companies. When we do, there are three key effects:

- it benefits companies that are truly ethical,
- it sends a clear message to corporations that enough is enough,
- it allows our money to become real currency – we are using it to vote against companies that employ child labour, use sweatshops, disregard indigenous communities, and cause environmental destruction.

5 You could organise an awareness-raising weekend at your church or youth group

Here's the possible shape of your weekend:

Friday evening: *Prayer focus*
Organise a creative prayer evening using resources from the Tearfund Lift the Label website (see bottom of page). Prayer will be focused on workers, the retail companies, other consumers and the Lift the Label campaign. You could begin with a prayer walk around your high street. Adapt some of the activities from this session.

Saturday: *Don't Shop Quietly Campaign launch*
Blitz the target stores on your high street with as many Lift the Label customer comment cards as possible. These are available to download on the site.

Sunday: *Challenge the church*
Hold a Lift the Label service, where there's a talk and a showing of the Lift the Label video. Organise a petition and collect signatures. Or take a short slot in your service to give a presentation.

PS What about boycotts?

Boycotts are tricky. They only really tend to work when they are the express wish of the workers we are trying to support. Sadly, when Western customers boycott stores, companies sometimes pull out of a country or a factory, resulting in many job losses. For workers in developing countries, any job is better than no job; so it's better to keep shopping and asking questions, to keep the pressure up and use your consumer power.

Tearfund's **Lift the Label** campaign has seen thousands of shoppers join the dots between what they believe and what they wear. All the resources you need can be found at http://youth.tearfund.org/lift+the+label

7 Are we nearly there yet?

Exodus 16:4–30

A session about our journey

Have we conquered injustice? Is this world free from oppression? Have we prised back the grip of poverty?

Today one third of the world's population lives on less than £1 per day; one in six people lacks access to clean water; and one person dies from an AIDS-related illness every 12 seconds. It is clear that we still have more to do. Are we nearly there yet? Not at all.

There are times when the journey ahead of us can seem a little overwhelming. Yet a look at the Bible reveals plenty about how, why and where our travels are taking us.

 Getting connected

Loaf

You will need: a photocopy of **Loaf** (pages 46,47) cut into slips; a piece of bread or small bread roll and a plate for each member of the group.

Give each person a slice of bread and a plate and divide the verses among the group, placing the slips of paper on the plate along with the bread. Read the passage aloud, each person reading what's on their slips in the correct order. (Don't let people eat the bread yet!)

Or

Map

You will need: felt-tip pens; photocopies of a map of the Middle East. Either use the one provided (page 39) or download one from the Internet: maps.google.com is a good place to look.

Give each person or pair their own map and ask them to plot what they think was the route taken by the Israelites on their journey from Egypt to Canaan. The journey as recorded in the Bible begins at Exodus 12:37. Compare results. (You can find the likely route at www.bible-history.com/maps/route_exodus.html)

 Living Scripture – Exodus 16:4–30

Read the passage together – unless you chose to read it during the **Loaf** activity earlier.

We'll start with a little background to the passage. It's one month on from their dramatic escape from Egypt and we could perhaps assume that the Israelites are now getting used to the reality of their situation; the buzz having worn off, their minds now turn to their physical needs. Back in chapter 15 they were complaining of their thirst, and now they're feeling more than a little peckish.

1. We see how, when their survival appears threatened, some react with fear while others find it easier to trust God. We see how God's help arrives – yet shrouded in mystery. Even the name they give their divine help – manna – illustrates this. Though God's commands are explicit and thorough, some still choose to disobey. Can you see any parallels between this phase of the exodus and our lives or society today?

2 God's perspective on the journey was surely different from that of the Israelites. For them it was a lengthy trek towards safety and a new home. Think about God's alternative agenda as a member of the group reads out loud Deuteronomy 8:2,3. It might seem like a foolish question, but why did God want to test his people? What did it matter to him whether or not they kept his commands? What was the destination he wanted for them?

3 Read Exodus 6:2–8 for more revelation about this point in history. A key word is 'know/known'. The suggestion here is that Abraham and Jacob didn't fully know God. Do you find that surprising? How do you feel about the wandering Israelites being on course for an 'upgraded' experience of the Lord?

Note: We define knowledge differently in our time. When we 'know' someone or something it is bound up with ideas of our being able to define or describe. Our knowledge is more abstract and theoretical than that pursued by the ancient Israelites. For them, to 'know' someone or something was to encounter, to experience fully and make a connection with. So, to know God would not mean that they could define him, but that they would share his concerns, that they would respond as he would respond to the world around them. It's because of this that Exodus 6:7 invokes the language of marriage as God binds himself to his people in covenant.

4 So if God led the Israelites out of slavery towards the Promised Land so that they might not only be safe but also experience a deeper, more intimate and profound relationship with him, what does that mean for us? Is the offer still on the table?

5 Take a quick look at John 6. What are the connections between this passage and the exodus? In particular, what do you make of John 6:32–40? How is Jesus 'the bread of life'? Is eating the bread of life the way to 'know' God?

6 How are we doing on our journey – our exodus from slavery towards freedom? How much have we taken advantage of the phenomenal offer of the chance to 'know' God, to share his concerns, his cares and his passions?

 Reaching out

Changing lives in India
Give out photocopies of **Changing lives in India** (page 67) and read it through quietly before discussing your views.

Possible responses, now and ongoing:
– Of course, India is not the only country where there is sexual exploitation of vulnerable people; nor is it the only place with an AIDS problem. What can you find out as a group about the extent of the issues on a global basis? And on a national level? And even a local level?

– Let the research you gather inform your prayers as a group. Is there any practical commitment that seems appropriate, however challenging?

 Touching God

Bread and water meditation
You will need: pieces of bread or small bread rolls (already at hand if you chose the **Loaf** icebreaker); a jug of water and some glasses; photocopies of **The Bread of Life Script** (page 45).

Place the bread and water centrally in the room, visible to everyone. Keep silence for two or three minutes as everyone takes an opportunity to pray and reflect on what they have heard and thought about. Then hand out the photocopies and invite a strong reader to lead everyone through the meditation, speaking slowly and pausing frequently where appropriate.

To finish, share the bread and water among you, drinking and eating as a reminder of God's total faithfulness. If you wish, and with the agreement of your church leadership, you could instead finish with communion.

Digging deeper

Give out copies of **Takeaway 7** (page 74), encouraging people to read it before the next session.

The Bread of Life Script

Leader:

Where are you on your own journey of faith?

Are you sensing the joy of release from captivity?

Are you grumbling in the desert, trapped by fear and mistrust of God?

Are you anxious about your daily needs? Your security?

Are you happy to wait for whatever it is that God will provide?

Are you struggling to believe that Jesus really could be the answer to your most pressing questions and needs?

Are you confident that your faith has the power to feed and nourish you?

Are you in pursuit of cerebral knowledge of the divine… or longing for a deeper relationship with your heavenly Father?

Talk to him about whatever's on your heart.

Or is your mind on the story of changed lives in India? There are times when compassion takes root within us and catches us unaware.

If you are feeling stirred by what you have heard and read, use this time to ask God what he might want you to do. What tools and resources do you have or can you seek out?

Together:

Father,

    hallowed be your name,

    your kingdom come.

Give us each day our daily bread

Forgive us our sins

    for we also forgive everyone who sins against us.

And lead us not into temptation.

Amen.

Loaf

4 Then the LORD said to Moses, "I will rain down bread from heaven for you. The people are to go out each day and gather enough for that day. In this way I will test them and see whether they will follow my instructions."

5,6,7 "On the sixth day they are to prepare what they bring in, and that is to be twice as much as they gather on the other days." So Moses and Aaron said to all the Israelites, "In the evening you will know that it was the LORD who brought you out of Egypt, and in the morning you will see the glory of the LORD, because he has heard your grumbling against him. Who are we, that you should grumble against us?"

8 Moses also said, "You will know that it was the LORD when he gives you meat to eat in the evening and all the bread you want in the morning, because he has heard your grumbling against him. Who are we? You are not grumbling against us, but against the LORD."

9,10 Then Moses told Aaron, "Say to the entire Israelite community, 'Come before the LORD, for he has heard your grumbling.'" While Aaron was speaking to the whole Israelite community, they looked toward the desert, and there was the glory of the LORD appearing in the cloud.

11,12 The LORD said to Moses, "I have heard the grumbling of the Israelites. Tell them, 'At twilight you will eat meat, and in the morning you will be filled with bread. Then you will know that I am the LORD your God.'"

13,14 That evening quail came and covered the camp, and in the morning there was a layer of dew around the camp. When the dew was gone, thin flakes like frost on the ground appeared on the desert floor.

15,16 When the Israelites saw it, they said to each other, "What is it?" For they did not know what it was. Moses said to them, "It is the bread the LORD has given you to eat. This is what the LORD has commanded: 'Each one is to gather as much as he needs. Take an omer for each person you have in your tent.'"

17,18 The Israelites did as they were told; some gathered much, some little. And when they measured it by the omer, he who gathered much did not have too much, and he who gathered little did not have too little. Each one gathered as much as he needed.

19,20 Then Moses said to them, "No one is to keep any of it until morning." However, some of them paid no attention to Moses; they kept part of it until morning, but it was full of maggots and began to smell. So Moses was angry with them.

21,22 Each morning everyone gathered as much as he needed, and when the sun grew hot, it melted away. On the sixth day, they gathered twice as much—two omers for each person—and the leaders of the community came and reported this to Moses.

23 He said to them, "This is what the LORD commanded: 'Tomorrow is to be a day of rest, a holy Sabbath to the LORD. So bake what you want to bake and boil what you want to boil. Save whatever is left and keep it until morning.'"

24,25,26 So they saved it until morning, as Moses commanded, and it did not stink or get maggots in it. "Eat it today," Moses said, "because today is a Sabbath to the LORD. You will not find any of it on the ground today. Six days you are to gather it, but on the seventh day, the Sabbath, there will not be any."

27,28 Nevertheless, some of the people went out on the seventh day to gather it, but they found none. Then the LORD said to Moses, "How long will you refuse to keep my commands and my instructions?"

29,30 "Bear in mind that the LORD has given you the Sabbath; that is why on the sixth day he gives you bread for two days. Everyone is to stay where he is on the seventh day; no one is to go out." So the people rested on the seventh day.

8 Does my faith look big in this?

Proverbs 29:7; Amos 8:4–6

A session about what we wear

A few years ago a book was published arguing that God loves fashion. It traced the sartorial trail through the Bible, suggesting that since God had made this world in all its splendour, we too ought to opt for fine threads and elegant gowns.

It never occurred to me that the book was touching on anything significant or even truly serious. It seemed that the only controversial thing about the subject was the depth of the neckline or size of the shoulder pads.

Today, things are different. Today we're waking up to the fact that faith and fashion go hand in hand – but not quite for the reasons previously suggested. These days we're aware of a far more important 'spiritual' issue: what happens to the people who make our clothes. The simple – and often uncomfortable – truth is this: when we snap up a bargain, all too often there are others around the world who are paying the price.

 Getting connected

Changing

In advance, agree that everyone will bring along one or two items from their wardrobe that they just don't wear. Maybe it was an unwanted gift or bought in a moment of madness! Pile them in the middle of the room. Select two people to have a race to see who can get dressed first. It's probably best if they leave their normal clothes on underneath, but you can vary the other rules as you see fit. For example, you could make them do it blindfolded, or with one arm in a sling. Be adventurous!

Or

Guesstimate Quiz 2

You will need: photocopies of the quiz (page 37); pens.

Give everyone five minutes to write their answers in the boxes and then compare your results. Who got the closest?

Answers:

1 £400

2 30

3 90 per cent

4 25 per cent

5 15p per hour

 Living Scripture – Proverbs 29:7; Amos 8:4–6

1 Read Amos 8:4–6. Speaking to the corrupt businessmen of the day, Amos comes up with five marks of a business that is bound to be on the wrong side of God. First up there's the fact that they couldn't wait to get the trade-free Sabbath and festival days over and done with so that

they could get back to business. Then there's the line about 'skimping the measure ... and cheating with dishonest scales'. What are the other three examples of bad practice?

2   Amos' talk of trading on the Sabbath might remind us of current multinationals and big chain stores that open for as much time as they can. What about the other four criticisms – are there any links between what Amos criticised and what we are used to today?

3   What did the writer of Proverbs think? Can you think of any proverbs relating to justice in the world of work?

4   What would Jesus' view be? Check out Luke 10:7. Can you think of any other verses which help us know what Jesus thought about the way we should treat workers?

5   We don't know how Jesus shopped, but we do know how he treated people. Think of any Bible accounts that you know about how he treated those he was meeting for the first time, particularly those looked down on by society's more powerful movers and shakers.

6   Is your local community at all concerned about workers' rights? Can you think of any examples of current issues? Of best practice? Of exploitation?

 Touching God

You will need: one or more photocopies (depending on the size of your group) of **Four workers** (pages 50,51), cut into sections and pasted onto card; some blank postcard-sized cards (enough for two or three each); pens; some assorted garments folded to show the labels recording their countries of origin.

Spread out the workers' stories around a table or the floor with a handful of blank cards and pens next to each one and one or two of the garments.

Get people to look at the care labels on their clothes and say where their garments were made.

Then give people time to move around and read each story. When each person has finished reading, encourage them to take a blank card, write a prayer and place it next to the story.

 Reaching out

Give out photocopies of **Action to protect clothing workers** (centre spread) and read it through quietly before discussing your views.

Possible responses, now and ongoing:
–   Are there any actions from the sheet that you (on your own or as a group) could take on? Discuss how to begin.

–   A thought-provoking book to study on this topic as a group would be *Beauty* in the Connect Bible Studies series published by Scripture Union.

 Digging deeper

Give out copies of **Takeaway 8** (page 75), encouraging people to read it before the next session.

Four workers

Dewi

Dewi knows just how much control retailers really have over their suppliers. She knows the hypocrisy of corporate giants who claim to value their labour yet turn a blind eye to the malevolent actions of the contractors. She knows all this because she has worked in several garment factories in Indonesia. She has experienced what it is like to work full time – a six-day week when it's less busy, seven days  otherwise – and still take home less than £50 each month. She has endured verbal abuse when trying to sit down after standing for ten hours at a machine. She knows what it is to start work at seven o'clock in the morning and finish at six the next morning when the company has a backlog of orders to fulfil.

'Eight years' working,' says Dewi, 'has taught me about the suffering and pain of workers in garment factories.'

The pain is real and the scars are visible.

'I have a friend who worked in the factory who severed her finger on the cutting machine. The machine was broken and couldn't be stopped, and there was no guard around the blade. In another factory, two pregnant workers miscarried in the toilet. They didn't tell the company they were pregnant because they were afraid of losing their jobs and they needed the money. They carried on working.

'You can't win. If you don't meet the target you lose out, but if you hit it you lose out, too.'

Rokye

Rokye's work is dull, but not quite in the way we might understand. For us, dull is waiting a couple of minutes for a commercial break to pass or spending a couple of hours on a train. For Rokye, dull is sitting silent, cross-legged and barefoot on top of a long bench with lots of other people, hunched over, sewing diamanté beads onto denim jackets. There are no chairs and he can't shift  position if he gets uncomfortable. Each bead is tiny and has to be threaded before it is sewn onto the jacket. The work is tiring on the eyes, as Rokye has to hold the material up close to see what he is doing. He sews 315 beads onto each jacket, and when he has finished one jacket, he picks up another and starts again.

Suthasinee

Suthasinee used to work in a factory in Thailand, making clothes for major sportswear companies. After an eleven-hour day that included three hours of overtime, she ended up taking home just £3.50. She did this six days a week, often working until midnight. Inside the factory the heat was oppressive and the rest of the working conditions appalling: blocked fire exits, for example, and bullying managers constantly shouting at the workers to work harder and faster. But working harder and faster meant more accidents: sewing machine needles through fingers and metal splinters in eyes. The work was exhausting. Once she was at home, Suthasinee had too little energy and too little cash to go out and enjoy herself. She would have had to spend more than a week's wages to buy one of the shirts she made, which sell for more than £12 in the West. At last she took a stand against the poor working conditions. She was fired.

Shima

Shima is a 17-year-old Bangladeshi who left school when she was 13 even though she wanted to continue her studies. She was too poor to attend school; her family needed what little money she could earn to help them survive. She moved to the city and has been working in the factory for the last three years. There she makes buttonholes in jeans and jackets for 12 or 13 hours each day, six days a week in a baking-hot factory that has no fans. For her time, she gets 1,700 taka per month (just under £20). Just under a third of that amount goes on rent.

Shima lives in a slum, which is a dangerous place for a woman to be at night. Theft and rape are common – 31 garment workers were raped in the area in the space of one month. These women were simply walking home late at night from the factories, unable to afford public transportation due to their low wages.

9 Why does my wallet ache?

Matthew 6:19–34; 1 Timothy 6:3–19; James 5:1–5

A session about trade and hope

A wise Christian once commented that the last part of our lives to get converted is our wallets. It's a good point – and sadly all too true. Another guy I heard about was asked to mentor someone. He agreed only on the grounds that the person would bring his bank statements along to their first session. After all, claimed the mentor, what was the point in trying to live a better life if they weren't going to start anywhere other than the heart of the matter?

Our attitude to money is varied. Look around the group and the chances are that you will have a range of experiences represented: those who have plenty, those who have little, some caught up in debt, others a slave to savings, some who have healthy attitudes to money and others in need of help.

In this session we are going to explore some of the ways in which money can hinder – and help – our lives as followers of Christ. It's such an emotive topic that it's important to set the scene and ensure as best you can that people do not leave feeling condemned or harangued. We want to leave the issue of change to God and simply remain open to whatever's on offer for ourselves.

 Getting connected

Wallet search

What's in your purse/wallet? Take yours out and empty the contents. If you've not got it with you then talk about what you usually have. What do you carry because of necessity? What goes with you for sentimental reasons?

Or

Bargain hunt

Arrange in advance for each person to bring with them a bargain that they're particularly pleased with. It could be an item of clothing or a gadget – anything. Take it in turns to guess both what it should have cost and what was paid for it.

 Living Scripture – Matthew 6:19–34; 1 Timothy 6:3–19; James 5:1–5

1 Read or hand out copies of **Wallet wisdom** (page 54). Have these quotations got it right? Are they helpful? Does anyone have any personal experiences that relate to them?

2 The Bible has plenty to say about money – almost 2,500 verses on the matter. Divide the following passages between you, with people working in small groups or pairs:

> Matthew 6:19–24
> Matthew 6:25–34
> 1 Timothy 6:3–10
> 1 Timothy 6:17–19
> James 5:1–5

Invite the pairs to read through their allotted passage and prepare a two- or three-sentence breakdown of what it says about money and how it should – and could – have an impact on our lives today. Give everyone 10-15 minutes to prepare and then get them to share what they've discovered.

Reaching out

Give out photocopies of **Money matters** (page 55) and read it through quietly before discussing your views.

Possible responses, now and ongoing:
- We're all busy people. But which of the three areas listed should you seriously and prayerfully consider reassessing? Or maybe all three of them need closer investigation?

 Touching God

Spending review

You will need: photocopies of the **Spending review** (page 56); a flip chart or large sheet of paper; pens; background music such as Matt Redman's 'I Will Offer Up My Life' (from the album *Passion For Your Name*) or 'Everything' (on the album *Holding Nothing Back* by Tim Hughes).

Most of us, sadly, are a long way off having a truly healthy approach to money. Interestingly, both the UK and the US are in the top ten for both national income (GDP) and child poverty. We may be rich, but the gap between those with the most and those with the least is widening. There's another kind of widening gap, too. While many of us have more and more of what we consider we 'need', there's a growing poverty within us, a wider chasm that hungers for more.

Hand out the **Spending review** and give people a few minutes to complete it. Assure them that their answers won't be revealed to anyone. Next, invite them to add up the totals for each of the three columns.

What does this say about our spending patterns? This is all utterly unscientific, but you get the point. Column one gives you an idea of how much you spend on yourself. Column two shows how much you spend on others. Column three shows how much you spend on the poor. So, how did you do? Do you spend way more on yourself than on the poor? More on others than on yourself? The ultimate question is this: are you proud of your spending patterns? It's time to loosen the grip that we have on our wallets, as well as the grip that our materialistic culture has on our lives.

Next, put a line down the centre of the flip chart to make two columns. As a group, make a list in the first column of all the ways in which you get persuaded to buy things – such as TV ads, magazines, chatting with friends etc. Then in the other column list the ways in which you buy things: online purchases, credit cards, cash and so on.

Talk about the items on each list that you find you have the least control over. Why is that? How does it happen?

Finally it's time to pray about all this. How might God be leading you towards a more healthy – and holy – relationship with your finances? Give people time and space to consider this while playing some appropriate music.

 Digging deeper

Give out copies of **Takeaway 9** (page 76), encouraging people to read it before the next session.

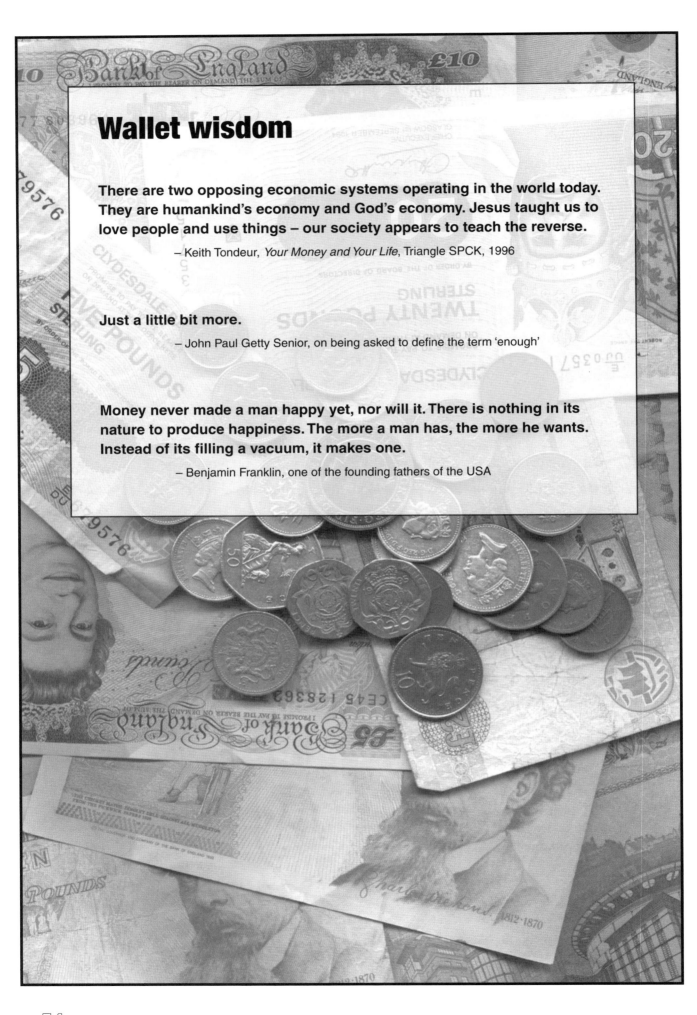

Wallet wisdom

There are two opposing economic systems operating in the world today. They are humankind's economy and God's economy. Jesus taught us to love people and use things – our society appears to teach the reverse.

– Keith Tondeur, *Your Money and Your Life*, Triangle SPCK, 1996

Just a little bit more.

– John Paul Getty Senior, on being asked to define the term 'enough'

Money never made a man happy yet, nor will it. There is nothing in its nature to produce happiness. The more a man has, the more he wants. Instead of its filling a vacuum, it makes one.

– Benjamin Franklin, one of the founding fathers of the USA

Money matters

Three practical ways in which we can all exercise a little more control over our funds:

1 Screen your bank's investments

How do you fancy investing in the arms trade? Are you up for providing financial backing to environmental polluters? What about giving a loan to an exploitative multi-national?

You may think I'm being offensive, but the truth is that by placing our money in some of our biggest high street banks we are involving ourselves in many of the above. Ask your bank about its CSR (Corporate Social Responsibility) policy. Ask where your investments are being targeted. If you don't get a good enough reply have a look at The Co-operative Bank (and Smile. co.uk, their online personal banking arm) or www.triodos.co.uk.

Will this have any impact? Well, you can take heart from history. The Quakers in the eighteenth century made a stand against the slave trade, refusing to invest money in any business linked to it. More recently banking boycotts were used to attack South Africa's apartheid, when California, for example, withdrew $50 billion from the country.

2 Make positive choices

As well as screening out the companies we don't approve of, we can make a choice to support those with positive values. By actively channelling our money into companies such as those with good labour practices and safety records, organic farms, alternative energy companies, or those who benefit local communities, we start to use our money for far better, bolder and brighter purposes.

A Fair Trade farmer can expect to get paid up to 500 per cent more for his coffee than a non-Fair Trade farmer. In a Fair Trade cooperative in Ghana, workers are paid 60 per cent more than the national wage. By supporting the system and opting for products that carry the Fair Trade logo we can invest in the lives of those whose access to the benefits of global trade would be otherwise restricted. It ensures decent wages and working conditions, as well as sound environmental practices. Whether it's your own kitchen or the one in your office or church, making a switch to Fair Trade coffee can, will and does make a tangible difference.

3 Examine your giving

Hypocrisy never looks good in Christians, but if our spending patterns inflict harm on others, it surely takes the edge off the positive impact of our giving. When there are 250 million child labourers worldwide, 100–200 million of them thought to be working in hazardous conditions such as using unsafe machinery, working in mines or inhaling fumes, something is wrong. There are eight million children worldwide involved in armed conflict, slavery and prostitution; and millions more caught up in cycles of poverty and abuse that appear almost impossible to break. These children are working for us. Give more away to charities and partners that help those living in poverty and you won't regret it.

Spending review

Put the answers to these questions in the grid below.

1 How much, typically, do you spend on a new pair of shoes?

2 How much did you spend on your family last Christmas?

3 How much do you give away at Christmas?

4 How much did you last spend at the hairdresser/ barber?

5 How much, typically, do you spend when you buy a present for a good friend?

6 How much, on average, do you put in the weekly church offering?

7 How much do you spend on junk food, snacks and ready meals during an average week?

8 How much, typically, would you spend on a night out?

9 How much did you give to the last charity appeal that you supported?

1	2	3
4	5	6
7	8	9

10 Where are God's fingerprints?

Psalm 65

A session about climate change, poverty and us

Why should Christians care for the environment? After all, isn't there a line back in Genesis about us ruling over and 'subduing' the earth? And isn't it true that all these rocks and rivers are just our temporary home, a pale reflection of the upgraded eternal glory yet to come?

For far too long we have bought into these distortions. We've seen the earth as something functional with little worth beyond its ability to sustain us. We have sniggered at 'tree huggers' and winced at 'earth mothers'. We may have allowed ourselves a quick chorus of 'All Things Bright and Beautiful', but only because the older members of the congregation liked it.

But not now. Things have changed. The groans and grief caused by a climate in chaos have finally reached our ears. The poetry and prose of Scripture has thawed our cynicism and opened our eyes. When the writer describes God looking at the earth and seeing that 'it was good', we are finally waking up to quite how big an understatement that good actually is.

 Getting connected

Treehug

You will need: a pile of plastic sandwich bags, enough for two or three each.

Go outside (into the garden where you are meeting, or the local park or green space nearby; in fact you could agree to start your session by meeting there) and, on your own, do as many of the following as you can in 10 minutes, weather permitting:

- climb a tree

- lie on the ground and stare at the sky

- collect some fallen leaves, bark fragments, twigs, moss, grass etc in a bag

- look for a wild flower

- watch an insect (collect it – live! – in a bag if you can)

- see if you can spot three different wild birds

- rub some soil between your fingers

- or anything else you can think of that connects you physically with the created world.

Come back together as a group and report what you did. Did you feel a little (or a lot?) embarrassed? So much the better; appreciating God may not always preserve our dignity!

Or

Nature pics

Arrange in advance for people to bring in a photograph or postcard of their favourite place to go to appreciate nature. It might be a holiday destination or a local park. Give people time to explain what it is they like about the place and why.

Living Scripture – Psalm 65

1   Read Matthew 10:29 and Psalm 65. How does God feel about his creation? How might he feel towards those who treat his creation with apathy and disdain?

2   God cares, too, about the people he has created; we were declared 'good' upon completion, just like the fish and plants and land and sea and sky. How do Psalm 139:13–15 and Romans 8:19,20 add to your understanding of this?

3   We should care for the created world because we were not made for isolation – either from each other or the elements which give us life. Remember how we were made 'in God's image'? Have a look at Jeremiah 10:12,13 and Colossians 1:16,17. How do these images of a God intimately connected with this world relate to us?

4   Climate change is a contentious issue – but it is not merely a political one. It is a profoundly theological issue. The way we treat the environment speaks volumes about the way we feel about God. And so much of climate change is linked to the deep concerns of our day. For example, we burn more fuel travelling further to work yet there are social problems caused by our increasing disconnection from our communities and friends. Can you think of other ways in which our changing climate is a symptom of a society at odds with its Creator?

 ## Touching God

You will need: bags of natural objects from **Treehug** or pictures from **Nature pics**; blank pieces of card; felt-tip pens.

If you've done the **Treehug** activity, then lay out whatever you brought back with you in the middle of the room. If you opted for **Nature pics**, then spread them out instead.

Give everyone a blank card and a pen. Choose one of the verses you looked at in **Living Scripture** that had an impact on you, write it out, and add the collection of verses to the display.

After a short silence, take time to pray one-sentence prayers about anything that comes to mind… gratitude to God for creation, thankfulness for your local environment, praise for landscapes of natural beauty you've been privileged to visit.

 ## Reaching out

Give out photocopies of **Update / Climate change / On the edge** (page 60) and read it through quietly before discussing your views.

Possible responses, now and ongoing:

–   Join Tearfund in a 40-day carbon fast. Get in touch and they'll send you a pack with 40 clear, simple and easily accessible daily actions you can get stuck into. Visit www.tearfund.org/ Carbonfast for all the information you'll need.

–   Organise a viewing of Al Gore's documentary *An Inconvenient Truth* and invite your local community. You can download notes to help work through the issues from the Tearfund website.

Digging deeper

Give out copies of **Takeaway 10** (page 77), encouraging people to read it before the next session.

MEMO: **Update / Climate change / On the edge**

The details of climate change are shocking. We find ourselves on the edge of a cliff – still able to retreat to relative safety, but in danger of getting swept away if we stay here much longer.

Scientists are increasingly united in their agreement about global warming and climate change: it's happening, and our obsession with burning fossil fuels is the reason why. Since the Industrial Revolution began more than 150 years ago the average global surface temperature has risen by 0.76 °C, much of that rise happening in the last 40 years. The links are obvious: the more coal and oil we've been burning to generate electricity and power for our technologically-advanced lifestyle, the more carbon has been emitted, trapping heat in the atmosphere and causing global temperatures to rise.

So what next? Well, if our emissions do not change then average global temperatures could rise by 2–3 °C in the next 50 years. By this time next century our great grandchildren will be looking back on a 5–6 °C rise and living in a world plunged into chaos of cinematic proportions.

Scientists are confident that a rise of just two degrees on the old, pre-Industrial Revolution average temperature is enough to cause significant damage to our climate. And guess who would bear the brunt of these changes? That's right – the poor. There is a very real danger that if temperatures rise 2 °C above the average that four billion people could be left facing growing water shortages; agriculture could be a not-so-distant memory in places like the tropics; while millions more will be left hungry. In Africa the result of this rise could be that between 40 and 60 million more people will find themselves exposed to malaria. The risk of melting ice sheets in Greenland and the West Antarctic rises significantly. Floods and droughts will become more extreme and more widespread, leaving those that are the most vulnerable on the planet with even less hope of survival.

But this is not the end of the story. There is still time, and while there is time there is hope. If we cut down our own carbon emissions as well as persuade the politicians to join in, we might just be able to avoid catastrophe. World leaders must agree to keep global temperature rise as far below 2 °C as possible and commit to the necessary binding targets to reduce emissions. We want them to allocate enough money to support vulnerable countries as well as to make it clear how they are going to slow down the rise in temperature.

Hope in Uganda

As Uganda's history gradually releases its grip on the country, new stories are emerging. Poverty, HIV and AIDS, grieving children left in charge of their younger siblings – these are some of the themes common to many throughout the country. Yet there are other players too; there's hope from local churches as they commit themselves to putting faith into action among those in greatest need.

Edith Wakumire knows about both sides of life in Uganda. As executive director and founder of the Uganda Women Concern Ministry (UWCM), she has held fast to the belief that communities can be mobilised through a network of volunteers recruited from local churches. She knows that, together, churches and communities can overpower the poverty and grief that surround the poor, the marginalised and disadvantaged.

It all started in a garage. It was 1992 and a few square metres were all that was needed for UWCM to take its first steps. Today, the Tearfund partner has 450 volunteers. The garage is just a distant memory replaced by fresh stories of transformation and sacrifice, as local churches are mobilised to take action.

Among those who benefit are children orphaned by HIV. Uganda's extended family network simply cannot support the increased number of child orphans, so in response UWCM has set up small centres to support both children and their grandparents. At each centre there is a Christian who will pray with the families, alleviating both spiritual and material poverty.

Abadu – his Muslim name – has also benefited from the work started by Edith. When he was diagnosed with HIV his fear of stigma caused him to leave his family and home. Fortunately he came into contact with UWCM. Desperately ill from HIV infection, he was given treatment. Today he is alive, well and the proud owner of a new name that he has chosen for himself: Christopher.

For Edith the work of UWCM draws inspiration from the direct simplicity of Jesus' words in Matthew 25:36: 'I needed clothes and you clothed me, I was ill and you looked after me. I was in prison and you came to visit me.'

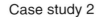

Breaking down barriers in Ethiopia

The work of Gotera Church in Ethiopia's capital Addis Ababa is remarkable and effective – and wrapped around a storyline that stays with the imagination for days.

It all starts with the city. Addis is not wealthy, but certain districts are poor – properly poor. Thousands live without water or electricity; jobs are things which belong to other people in other areas. Yet the massive migration of families from rural areas to the city continues.

And then there's this one particular church – Gotera. For years it was one of the district's best kept secrets. Church members tried to avoid the world beyond its doors and, apart from occasional tours of duty out into the streets to preach, Gotera Church was hidden from view.

Then it happened: they got a visit from Mesfin, a development worker from their denomination. He told them Bible stories, sparked off discussions and opened their eyes to the possibility that all these barriers between them and their community might not be such a good thing after all.

The first step, Mesfin suggested, was to get out and visit unchurched people in their homes, to ask about their concerns and listen to what they had to say. At first, out of the 40-strong congregation, just one overcame the fear and took up the challenge. Gradually others followed, returning with a sense of shock – their own poverty dwarfed by what they had seen among the widows, orphans and outcasts around them. It was time to act.

Within months the church family had visited 600 households – not preaching, but listening, learning and inviting others to join together for a community meeting. There they decided to identify and work with the 200 poorest households, most of which were headed by women.

What followed next was simple, yet life changing. The church helped group these 200 households into ten self-help groups, appointing two part-time community workers to support, train and advise. The groups worked, raised funds and saved together. And, as their funds increased, so too did their confidence and self-esteem.

Within six months there was enough money saved to start supporting women as they put business ideas into practice.

One set up a roadside tea shop; another bought, farmed and sold a cow. One group even made a 'loan' to one of their members dying of HIV to buy medicines, even though the money will never be paid back.

The stories of the good that came out of this one church's decision to open up the doors and serve its neighbours go on and on. Tearfund is proud to stand alongside them, to support and cheer them on. But Tearfund also wants to be a part of the action, breathing life and change into more communities, uniting to tackle the material and spiritual poverty that plague our world.

Case study 3

Filling empty hands in Malawi

Let me tell you about Harry. He's a pastor in a small village somewhere down below the equator – Malawi, to be precise. Anyway, Harry had five cows. No, this isn't a joke and it's not a maths puzzle either; it's just a true story about a pastor with five cows.

So, he had these cows. They were his entire livelihood. Harry, his wife and his five kids relied on their cattle. But one day there were only four. No warning signs, no illness, no 'I'm off to find a better life' note scratched in the dirt. Just one dead cow lying on the ground. It was a big deal.

A while later the big deal became an even bigger deal: another cow was found dead. This time there were signs: a wound in the animal's side, a flow of blood marking the exit of life from this innocent animal.

It was a deliberate attack. Harry was left with just three cows.

This crisis was the source of every conversation throughout the village. The people were shocked. Harry knew all eyes were fixed on him, their pastor. How would he react?

He forgave. He was tempted not to, of course. But he forgave the killer of his cows and people looked on in surprise. His loss became others' gain, as villagers were intrigued by Harry's reaction and took a fresh interest in his faith.

There's a point to this story and it's not about cows or poverty. But it is about you and me and Harry and how we all interact with the people around us.

Harry's actions challenged a core belief in the people which was like a set of chains around their ankles, holding them back, hurting them.

This is how Harry himself explained it: 'In the village there was a belief that if I am lacking then I cannot assist anyone. But we told people that in the midst of lacking there is still something that I can assist my friend with.'

With what they'd seen of Harry's response to his loss and some training and support from their local Tearfund partner, this message of hope and help took hold. The church took courage. They pooled what little resources they had to rebuild the home of an elderly blind man in the village. Later they bought a school uniform for a girl from a poor family. Then they repaired the roof for an old woman.

Their eyes had been opened, their hearts changed and the lives of all in the village improved.

All it took was a couple of dead cows and a faithful man who refused to give in to fear and anger.

Tackling trade in people in Cambodia

Sorn Srey Him is 15 and lives in Cambodia. Last year she was the victim of human trafficking, lured to Thailand with the promise of a well paid job and a brighter, better future. The reality was far from it: Srey Him ended up spending a month in a Thai prison, caged along with five other illegal immigrants. Some were raped, some were beaten. She managed to buy her way out of the prison, but the horrors of the past are never far away from her.

Two centuries after the abolition of the slave trade, at least 12 million people are trapped in forced labour with as many as 2.4 million of them the victims of human trafficking. Of those trafficked, 80 per cent are women and girls. Each year an estimated 1.2 million children are trafficked. From prostitution to begging, forced labour to military service, marriage or forced illegal adoption, the trade in people is big business.

The details of the human trafficking vary with each case, but there are certain similarities that draw many of the stories together. Often it starts, as it did with Srey Him, with people made vulnerable by poverty being deliberately misled. They are promised easy, safe work with decent pay – yet what they end up with is horribly different. At other times, people are simply taken by force to another country in which their vulnerability is exploited. Alone, illegal and impoverished, many people who have been trafficked feel as if they have no option other than to keep quiet and put up with the torment of a life of slavery.

But the story does not always end here. There are Tearfund partners working in various parts of the world to prevent trafficking and to rebuild the lives of those caught up in its misery. One of those partners is CHO (Cambodia Hope Organisation). Their work has a remarkable impact on the lives they touch. By working with whole families, training them in trades such as sewing or farming, CHO gets to the root causes of many people's vulnerability: poverty. Education about the issue is vital too, and CHO does a great job of spreading the message about the dangers posed by strangers who come and promise great jobs and great pay if families allow their children to travel over the border for work.

Dreams coming true in Bangladesh

Wars and international disputes always bring suffering to ordinary people; this is one of life's eternal truths. After the Bangladesh war of independence in 1971, thousands of Bihari people living as refugees in Dhaka were not allowed to return to Pakistan. Social exclusion and lack of formal citizenship in Bangladesh made it impossible for them to get work. They became yet another illustration of the consequences of war.

Back when peace was fragile, Tearfund's partner Heed Handicrafts was inspired to create employment opportunities for the Bihari people who might otherwise have been forgotten. The work was simple – handicrafts made from locally available resources – yet, more than 30 years on, an estimated 10,000 people have had access to training and employment as a result of Heed's activities. But it is not really about big statistics; it is about the changed lives of individuals. People like Nurul Islam Nuru.

As a boy, Nuru was a capable student with a dream of becoming a Master's graduate. However, he could not continue his studies; he realised that his father would not be able to provide food for his three younger brothers and four sisters on his small income. Nuru recalls, 'Many days my parents skipped their meals to provide food for us. It was very painful for me.'

Being the eldest son, Nuru felt the responsibility to work to help his father support the family and left his village for Dhaka. There he joined a small leather workshop as a trainee, in return for food and accommodation in the factory. 'As I slept in the factory I would dream that one day I would get a salary and would make my parents happy with my income.'

Even after his training the salary was poor, but Nuru continued patiently for 12 years, improving his skills and working hard. Then he heard about Heed Handicrafts through a friend and, within three years, was able to set up his own business employing 12 artisans, supplying leather goods around the world. Today he is finally able to support his family, as he had always dreamed, and to enable his daughter to have the schooling that he had to miss out on.

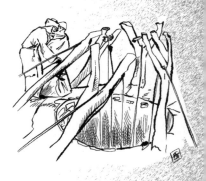

Caring for orphans in Uganda

Lawrence's life follows a script familiar to millions of children trapped by poverty and loss: each morning he wakes at six, organises the house so that water is fetched, food cooked and the house swept. After an hour-long walk to school he studies and returns home. Then he must organise food, collection of firewood and all the tasks associated with a house made up of four teenage boys. At times Lawrence – just 15 years old – has to sacrifice his day at school in order to look for work for which, if he's lucky, he will be paid. At least things are better now that his uncle is off the scene. He used to take the boys' clothes to sell, and help himself to whatever else he wanted.

Lawrence is one of a growing army of children in Uganda and across Africa whose parents died from AIDS-related illnesses. What will the future look like when they, as a generation of adults who lost their childhood, find themselves not just in charge of single homes, but of a whole nation?

But forget the theorising and the analysis for a moment; these are kids who have nursed their parents, who have seen them die and awoken the next morning to the reality that they are the ones who are now in charge. These are kids who miss their mum and dad.

Unsurprisingly, there are limited statistics available about the phenomenon of child-headed households. Like some mutation of Dickens' street urchins, these ex-children are forced to live by their wits, to act on survival instincts that lead them into the shadows and away from public gaze. Perhaps too, the reality is just all a bit much for us: a society that relies on orphans to care for orphans is surely only holding on to civilisation by a thread. One slip and things could get a whole lot worse.

The good news is that, for some, things are getting better.

Lawrence and his family have been helped by their headmaster, John.

'They are orphans. Their father was my neighbour. I give them money to go to hospital and some money for food. It's my initiative as a human being.'

John understands the importance of education for those orphaned by AIDS: 'If they have knowledge they'll be able to maintain themselves, to stand on their own. I want to help them get an education.'

With 67 orphans out of 400 pupils in his school, John is fighting to rewrite the future for young people like Lawrence. And it costs him too, as he chooses to pay their school fees and buy their uniforms himself – less than £10 each year, but a significant amount to a Ugandan school teacher. Tearfund partner TAIP is supporting John and others like him seeking to help orphans.

Changing lives in India

It took many miles, years and lessons to change the Israelites from slaves to people with the freedom to act as God wanted.

Changing lives takes time. That's what Tearfund has experienced in Mumbai, India, where partner Sahaara Charitable Society (SCS) works closely with the Gateways Ministry International (GMI) group of churches to transform the present and the future for Mumbai's commercial sex workers.

Over five years, charity staff and church volunteers have worked together to bring hope, freedom and everyday miracles into the city's seemingly impenetrable red light districts. There they have worked alongside the strong who use their influence to control and abuse others, as well as the vulnerable and powerless who are their victims.

This is no hit and run project. Instead the local church and charity unite to build relationships over the long term with those caught up in the sex trade. Over the last five years as many as 60 women and 15 children have benefited from the work. Ten women have quit the flesh trade and six children have been put into various homes finding fresh hope through the local church.

Of course there are people who do not welcome this work. The local pimps and brothel owners lose out when the local church and Tearfund partner put the gospel into action like this. Sex workers can find themselves at risk of retribution and physical danger when they try to leave their clutches. Pimps and brothel owners are encouraged to allow the women and children to move on and the church and charity work hard to develop relationships with these powerbrokers.

Through prayer, courage and commitment to the hard work of building relationships, the members of the GMI churches and Sahaara Charitable Society are changing lives, unlocking the transformative power of the gospel. The vision to stop the spread of AIDS by 2015 in several countries where Tearfund partners work relies on projects like this.

Takeaway 1

What's wrong with the world?

Read Naaman's story in 2 Kings 5, which illustrates the potential our actions hold – both good and bad. A fine warrior became offended when Elisha's suggested cure for leprosy failed to match his expectations.

Think about it:

It's easy for us to become narrow in our thinking about how God should work – and it is then just a small step to becoming offended when God behaves differently.

We make this world about what we can get, what we can consume, what we can taste… all the time reducing its size. We make our world too small, our horizons too limited, our sun too pale. The materialist on his deathbed knows this; his life's pursuit of gain and greed is finally revealed as nothing but a waste.

What's wrong with the world is often what's wrong with us. More importantly, the reverse is also true: our hands hold considerable potential for incredible good.

Namaan ends up being noted for his generosity rather than his arrogance (see verse 23). What are the chances of us being remembered for the same reasons?

My response:

_____

_____

_____

_____

_____

_____

_____

_____

_____

_____

Takeaway 2

What's so special about God's kingdom?

Read Exodus 3:7–10. The Israelites in captivity under Pharaoh in Egypt found themselves at the wrong end of a power system designed to protect the interests of those at the top. Fortunately for us, God's plans were bigger than the Egyptian restrictions, as Moses found out.

Think about it:

It all starts off pretty well, with God apparently building up to some blockbuster action sequence where he takes the Egyptians apart, piece by piece. As God declares that he has 'seen the misery… heard the crying' and has 'come down to rescue them,' surely Moses would have been rubbing his hands in eager anticipation! Then come four words that turn the tables completely: 'I am sending you.' God unexpectedly places Moses at the heart of his Plan A. Of course Moses was unable to achieve the task; of course it was a ridiculous idea; of course Moses would be utterly dependent on God for success.

Can you still hear that call today? We know that God sees current miseries, tears and suffering. Can you become the 'you' at the heart of his plan?

My response:

_____

_____

_____

_____

_____

_____

_____

_____

_____

_____

_____

Takeaway 3

Where do we fit in all this?

Schindler, Abraham… We started out looking at the idea of the ways in which we can plead for each other. But what we haven't yet touched on is the idea of how Jesus fits in to all this.

> **"My dear children, I write this to you so that you will not sin. But if anybody does sin, we have one who speaks to the Father in our defence – Jesus Christ, the Righteous One."**
>
> 1 John 2:1

Flick back to Luke's account of Jesus' final hours on the cross and we find a powerful example of Christ speaking in our defence:

> **Jesus said, "Father, forgive them, for they do not know what they are doing."**
>
> Luke 23:34

Think about it:

What does his extraordinary request tell us about the character of Jesus? And what about us? How does this image of Christ as advocate – in the midst of his own brutal torture – impact us? He joins us in the place where we deserve judgement, yet urges God to be gracious.

Does this have anything to say about how we should look out for others? Personal troubles and pain did not stop Jesus from looking out; how do we treat others when we're gripped by sorrow and stress?

My response:

_____

_____

_____

_____

_____

_____

_____

 Takeaway 4

What's holding us back?

Have a look at Matthew 6:19–34 and see what Jesus had to say about our attitude to possessions, appetites and anxiety.

Think about it:

Imagine Jesus is saying the words of these verses directly to you, sitting in a chair opposite you in your own home. If it helps, read the abbreviated version of the words again, this time from *The Message*.

> **"It's obvious, isn't it? The place where your treasure is, is the place you will most want to be, and end up being ... You can't worship God and Money both ... There is far more to your life than the food you put into your stomach, more to your outer appearance than the clothes you hang on your body ... Give your entire attention to what God is doing right now, and don't get worked up about what may or may not happen tomorrow."**

– Do these words of Jesus have an impact?

– Do they prompt you to think about your own life?

– Do they leave you mulling over the possibility of making some changes?

My response:

_____

_____

_____

_____

_____

_____

_____

_____

_____

_____

Which way is up?

Our shopping – whether it's for clothes, food or a decent bank to take care of our money – is an incredibly powerful tool. It can bag us great bargains… and help perpetuate the cycle of abuse and oppression that leaves many in the developing world picking up the tab for our western lifestyles. Or it can promote justice and freedom, acting as a genuinely good tool for our faith. Visit http://youth.tearfund.org/lift+the+label/ to find out more.

Think about it:

During the week, mull over these words of Martin Luther King Jnr, who pointed out that connection comes with a responsibility, whether we like it or not:

> 'We will have to repent in this generation not merely for the cruel words and actions of the bad people, but for the appalling silence of the good people.'

How could acting on this impact your shopping habits?

My response:

_____

_____

_____

_____

_____

_____

_____

_____

_____

_____

_____

Takeaway 6

How loudly do we have to sing?

Leviticus 25 lays out the blueprint for a unique approach to wealth and society: the Year of Jubilee. Try to get your head around the details; the bulk of the info appears in verses 8–19.

The concept has never really been put into action. There have been years called 'jubilee' over the centuries, but none have ever been as radical as Leviticus suggests.

Think about it:

— What would society look like today if we followed such a pattern?

— How do you think our lives/ our homes/ our church services would differ if every 50 years we were all brought back to an economic level playing field?

— Are there issues we are facing today that might be helped in a society that practised biblical jubilee?

My response:

_____

_____

_____

_____

_____

_____

_____

_____

_____

_____

_____

_____

_____

Are we nearly there yet?

Find out about the needs of your local area. A look through your local paper should reveal some of the current problems and initiatives. There might be other needs that you are aware of.

Think about it:

Could God be calling you or your small group or your church to get involved in meeting any of these local needs?

Reflect on these quotes from *Sharing Jesus* by the late Rob Frost (published 2008, Scripture Union):

Evangelism is far more credible when Christians
are willing to enter into the sufferings of the world.

A church cut off from its community
is like a tree cut off from its roots – weak and barren!

If personal evangelism is to be effective,
it must be set in the context of real, caring human relationships.

My response:

_____

_____

_____

_____

_____

_____

_____

_____

Takeaway 8

Does my faith look big in this?

Here are the main principles included in the code of practice put out by the Ethical Trading Initiative. Think about how they relate to biblical principles.

- No one should be forced to work.

- Workers should be able to join and form trade unions.

- Working conditions should be safe and healthy.

- Child labour shall not be used.

- Working hours should not be excessive.

- Wages should be enough to live on and provide some discretionary income.

- Workers should be treated equally, regardless of their sex, ethnic group, religion or political opinions.

- Where possible, workers should be provided with regular employment.

- Workers should not be verbally, physically or sexually abused or disciplined.

Find out more from www.ethicaltrade.org

Think about it:

What is it about people working in the garment industry that leaves them so vulnerable to exploitation? Our love of cheap clothes encourages companies to put profits before people. As they look around for people to make these clothes, their eyes rest on the people who will make less of a fuss about putting up with bad conditions. People in the developing world have fewer choices and get caught up in what is known as the 'race to the bottom', where those governments and companies that win are the ones prepared to impose the toughest conditions on their workers.

My response:

_____

_____

_____

_____

_____

Why does my wallet ache?

More than one billion people live on less than 60p a day, with nearly half the world's population (2.8 billion) living on less than £1.10 a day.

Aid can make a massive difference to their daily lives – providing essentials like clean water and proper sanitation, medical centres, free education, better transportation systems and roads. In 2000, members of the United Nations agreed eight Millennium Development Goals (MDGs) to halve world poverty by 2015. Achieving these targets would lift millions of people out of poverty.

Yet not only are rich nations falling behind in working to achieve these goals, but frequently they attach conditions to how aid is spent rather than allowing developing countries to decide how best to spend it themselves.

The UK government currently gives just 0.34 per cent of its national income in aid, planning to reach 0.7 per cent by 2013. Sadly, this will be too late for millions of people dying of preventable diseases such as cholera, typhoid, worms, malaria and scabies, simply because they do not have access to safe drinking water or clean sanitation. If the UK met their 0.7 per cent target by 2008, an extra 1.5 million people could beat poverty. The MDGs are still achievable but only if countries honour their past and future promises.

Think about it:

Do you keep your promises? Sometimes we all fall short of our commitments. But God never does. He is 100 per cent committed to the poor and he asks us to be too. In Proverbs 31:9 God calls us to 'speak up and judge fairly; defend the rights of the poor and needy.' He hates injustice and poverty. We deny one another our true worth when we allow people to remain in poverty.

Tearfund is challenging the UK government not to delay a moment longer in meeting its target of 0.7 per cent in aid. What could you do? Well, you could set the government an example by giving at least 0.7 per cent of your own income to help meet vital needs in some of the poorest countries in the world and then ask the Chancellor of the Exchequer to match it.

Want to join in? Go to: http://youth.tearfund.org/lift+the+label/finance/aid-a+promise+for+life.htm

My response:

_____

_____

_____

_____

Takeaway 10

Where are God's fingerprints?

On your own, read through Job 38 and 39, out loud if you can. Regardless of all that strange stuff at the start when God barters with Satan, by the end the author's got fully into God's character.

Think about it:

Note the intricate detail the writer focuses on. How would you respond if God uttered those words to you? Would you go about your daily routine in quite the same way tomorrow if you'd been confronted with this level of detail about the world God loves?

My response:

_____

_____

_____

_____

_____

_____

_____

_____

_____

_____

_____

_____

_____

_____

_____

_____

_____

Other books in the Multi-Sensory series

* fresh * innovative * imaginative * inspirational * practical

MULTI-SENSORY CHURCH

Over 30 ready-to-use ideas for creative churches and small groups

Sue Wallace

MULTI-SENSORY PRAYER

Over 60 ready-to-use ideas for creative churches and small groups

Sue Wallace

MULTI-SENSORY SCRIPTURE

50 innovative ideas for exploring the Bible in churches and small groups

Sue Wallace

MULTI-SENSORY TOGETHER

15 ready-to-use sessions for Bible exploration in creative small groups

Ian Birkinshaw

MULTI-SENSORY SEASONS

15 ready-to-use Bible-based sessions through the seasons for creative small groups

Wendy Rayner and Annie Slade

MULTI-SENSORY PARABLES

15 ready-to-use sessions on the stories Jesus told – for creative churches and small groups

Ian Birkinshaw

MULTI-SENSORY PROPHETS

15 ready-to-use sessions on God's messengers – for creative churches and small groups

Mike Law

MULTI-SENSORY MESSAGE

Ready-to-use Bible-based activities on mission – for creative churches and small groups.

Dave Maclure

This series is just part of a wide range of resources for churches and small groups published by Scripture Union.

SU publications are available from Christian bookshops, on the Internet or via mail order. You can:

-     phone SU's mail order line: 0845 0706006
-     email info@scriptureunion.org.uk
-     log on to www.scriptureunion.org.uk
-     write to SU Mail Order, PO Box 5148, Milton Keynes MLO, MK2 2YX